Introducing
CITIZENSHIP

A HANDBOOK FOR PRIMARY SCHOOLS

DON ROWE

A & C Black • London

Reprinted 2001 (Twice)
First published 2001 by A & C Black (Publishers) Ltd
37 Soho Square, London W1D 3QZ

Copyright text © 2001 The Citizenship Foundation
Copyright illustrations © 2001 Michael Evans
Copyright photographs © 2001 The Citizenship Foundation
Copyright video © 2001 The Citizenship Foundation

ISBN 0-7136-5857-6

A CIP catalogue record for this book is available from
the British Library.

Printed by Caligraving Ltd, Thetford, Norfolk

Acknowledgements

This handbook is very much the result of team effort. During its development I have been able to draw on the assistance of a number of very experienced and committed colleagues.

I would like to thank Gill Rose who worked with the Citizenship Foundation on the handbook for a term and did much to ensure the quality of the video programme. Annabelle Dixon and Mark Prentice, both of whom epitomise the reflective practitioner, have done innovative work on critical thinking in primary schools. They each contributed sections to Chapter 3: Mark on structuring literacy work; Annabelle on the importance of identifying 'tool' words. I should also like to thank those members of the project's support team whose help and advice have been invaluable throughout, namely: Irene Fielding and Ann Kibby who, though over-worked head teachers, still found time to attend meetings and lend encouragement and support. Special thanks are due to Annette Mountford and Candida Hunt of Family Links and Elizabeth Hartley-Brewer for their expert advice on working with parents and families. Thanks also to Gill Morris of Camden LEA for contributing to the sections on whole school policy and school councils, and to Roy Honeybone of Hampshire LEA for commenting on the drafts.

The video programme would not have been possible without the heads and staff of a number of schools who were brave enough to let us record them at work. We found their idealism and professionalism extremely heartening. In particular, we thank Dilys Brotia, Natasha Wilson and Laurence Harding of Toriano Junior School, Camden; Glynis King, Chris Jay and Angela Bonsar of Bentley West Primary School, Walsall; Lilian Sanders and Sam Sillitto of Hazelgrove JMI School, Hertfordshire; and Tessa Moss of Wheatcroft JMI School, Hertfordshire. We especially thank those teachers who allowed us to record them at work but whom we were unable to include in the final programme. And very special thanks to the children of all these schools for the great pleasure their contributions to this programme have given us. We are especially grateful for the organisation and skill of Camilla Byk, of B.Y.K. Media, who so excellently and painstakingly produced the video.

Finally, my thanks to Jan Newton, chief executive of the Citizenship Foundation, who has worked with me on this project from the beginning and whose support and forbearance have been far more than one has a right to expect.

Don Rowe
Director, Curriculum Resources
Citizenship Foundation

British Telecommunications plc

The Citizenship Foundation gratefully acknowledges the generous support of BT in developing these training materials and the associated picture books.

Contents

Introduction

HOW TO USE THIS PACK

Created by the Citizenship Foundation, the *Introducing Citizenship* pack includes this practical handbook and a video. Four picture books in the *Thinkers* series have been written to be used with the pack and are available separately (see page 74).

The pack provides practical ideas for teaching citizenship at Key Stages 1 and 2 as well as an explanation of the underlying theory. The resources will be useful to primary teachers and subject coordinators, and will also be of interest to parents, whose understanding, input and support are also of great importance.

The handbook

This handbook provides practical teaching strategies to encourage children to explore the issues of citizenship and engage in critical thinking. This will enable them to participate confidently and more fully in the home, school, and wider communities to which they belong. The book also looks in detail at the theory of citizenship education and offers insights into recent research.

Chapter 1 looks at the theories underlying education for citizenship. It introduces the framework and key concepts and discusses how these relate to the social and moral development of children.

Chapter 2 looks at the vital importance of talk in citizenship work and discusses a number of ways to deepen the quality of discussion in class.

Chapter 3 examines the links between language, literacy and citizenship education, including how story books can be used as a stimulus for thinking, speaking and listening.

Chapter 4 discusses the contribution of the whole school experience to citizenship learning, with the aim of encouraging children to participate in school life and of involving parents in citizenship work.

Chapter 5 suggests questions and issues of teaching and learning which can be considered alongside the video in order to benefit fully from the video resource.

Appendices I and II contain a programme for school training sessions in citizenship, along with a questionnaire that was used with one of the classes featured on the video.

Appendix III provides footnotes to the text, suggests further reading, and gives details of organised courses that help parents and teachers to work together to support their children's social, emotional and intellectual growth.

The video

In the sixty-minute video accompanying this handbook, different teachers are seen working with classes in their own ways. Each teacher's understanding of the subject area influences how they select and address issues, ask questions, and involve the children in discussion or practical work.

In these real classroom situations, all the different aspects of theory come together in a dynamic interaction – everything is happening at once. Having such teaching practice on video provides an opportunity for analysis from different points of view, whether this be concerning the teacher's technique or the nature of the children's thinking. Three of the four sections of the video show children thinking and talking about citizenship issues. The final section shows school councils in action and demonstrates what a valuable contribution children can make when they participate more fully in school life.

Links between the video and chapters in the handbook

Section 1 The Citizenship Circle

- social and moral development: Chapter 1
- thinking skills: Chapter 2
- encouraging quality talk: Chapter 2
- different functions of questions: Chapter 2

Section 2 Weighing the Evidence
- Circle Time: Chapter 2
- open and closed questions: Chapter 2
- progression between key stages: Chapter 1

Section 3 Reading, Thinking, Speaking and Listening
- citizenship work and literacy: Chapter 3
- developing the language of citizenship: Chapter 3

Section 4 A Better Place
- whole school policies for citizenship: Chapter 4
- running school councils: Chapter 4

Using the pack flexibly

Introducing Citizenship has been designed to be used flexibly. It may be used as a resource by individual classroom teachers or to provide a basis for staff discussion and training purposes. The *Thinkers* picture books (see below) are a particularly useful starting point for applying the strategies outlined in Chapter 3. After which, the same strategies can be applied using a wide variety of other books. See page 34 for some recommended titles.

You may choose to watch the video and read the notes relevant to it in Chapter 5 of this handbook before turning to the more theoretical discussions in the earlier chapters and to familiarising yourself with the *Thinkers* stories. Alternatively, you may prefer to start by reading the first chapters of the handbook to enhance your understanding of the classroom sessions in preparation for watching the video and reading the *Thinkers*.

Either way, the pack will be of practical benefit both to classroom teachers and to those who have responsibility for training and supporting their colleagues in educating for citizenship.

THINKERS as starting points

The picture books in the *Thinkers* series are engaging stories with lively and appealing illustrations. Developed in conjunction with the Citizenship Foundation, these apparently simple open-ended stories provide a stimulating catalyst to the children's enthusiastic exploration of the complexities of familiar situations. As children talk and think about a story and its characters, and listen to the views of the other children, they will make connections to their own experience and expand their own understanding.

Each story raises a key issue which the children will soon have the confidence to define, discuss and explore, and to open out into associated issues. Questions at the back of each book can be used as starting points for discussion.

The key issues addressed by each of the *Thinkers* picture books are given in Chapter 3, page 33. To order copies of the books and this pack, full details are provided on the order form on page 75.

1. CITIZENSHIP AND THE PRIMARY CURRICULUM

THE KEY CONCEPTS

In 1999, the Government announced the framework for the new Curriculum 2000. For the first time ever, the curriculum was given an overarching statement of values, aims and purposes. The statement strongly emphasises that, in addition to the transmission of a wide range of knowledge and understanding, the school curriculum is based on a definable set of social values:

Education influences and reflects the values of society, and the kind of society we want to be. It is important, therefore, to recognise a broad set of common values and purposes that underpin the school curriculum and the work of schools...
Education is also a route to equality of opportunity for all, a healthy and just democracy, a productive economy, and sustainable development. Education

should reflect the enduring values that contribute to these ends. These include valuing ourselves, our families and other relationships, the wider groups to which we belong, the diversity in our society and the environment in which we live. Education should also reaffirm our commitment to the virtues of truth, justice, honesty, trust and a sense of duty.
National Curriculum Handbook, Key Stages 1 & 2, p 10.

These are the kinds of values that must underpin public life in a humane and democratic society. Within this social focus the curriculum must also develop the individual. The statement of values suggests that the curriculum should:

... develop principles for distinguishing right and wrong. It should develop [pupils'] knowledge, understanding and appreciation of their own and

different beliefs and cultures, and how these influence individuals and societies. The school curriculum should pass on enduring values, develop pupils' integrity and autonomy and help them to be responsible and caring citizens capable of contributing to the development of a just society.

As part of this task, schools should help pupils 'understand their responsibilities and rights'.

Education for citizenship is now identified as a major aim of education at all key stages. For many years, it was regarded as being more appropriate to the transmission of civic knowledge within secondary schools. However, it is now widely recognised that primary schools play a crucial role in establishing the foundations of positive citizenship.

THE IDEA OF CITIZENSHIP

Since the ancient Greeks, any person who has the right and the responsibility to participate democratically in society has been considered a **citizen**. But to think that young people only attain citizenship when they turn 18, gain the vote and take adult responsibilities, is to disregard many of the fundamental rights of citizenship, such as the right to freedom from physical attack and the right to be listened to. Children have many such rights from the first days of their lives and in this sense they are already citizens.

The general idea of citizenship is clear enough, yet there is no consensus about what makes the ideal citizen, nor about the relationship between the citizen

and the state. Some ideologies consider the community more important than its individual members, and emphasise **duties** rather than **rights**, whereas the main function of more liberal states is to ensure that individual citizens can flourish according to their own values and beliefs. For this to happen each citizen must have certain rights and freedoms which the state should not infringe. What binds individuals together is the idea of a social contract into which citizens freely enter. Socialisation and education are the primary means of inducting the young into such a society and motivating them to join in.

What kind of citizens should primary schools aim to develop?

When asked this question, primary teachers almost always make similar suggestions. They aim to develop citizens who will:

- care about what goes on in the community
- be able to express their opinions
- be socially confident
- develop a clear set of moral values
- be aware of their rights
- increasingly take responsibility for their actions
- be able to think for themselves
- respect others and the law
- be tolerant and respectful of diversity.

Such personal attributes or qualities help to make schools, as well as local and national communities, better for all their members. They are close to the heart of what schools mean by personal and social development; are essential components of education for citizenship; and are strongly reflected in the new framework for Personal, Social and Health Education (PSHE) and Citizenship. According to the official guidance, PSHE and Citizenship should:

a. develop personal effectiveness (e.g. self-confidence and responsibility)
b. prepare pupils to play an active role as citizens
c. encourage healthy and safe living
d. promote effective and fulfilling relationships based on respect for difference.

Each of these areas has an important bearing on the **rights** and **responsibilities** of the developing child.

Whilst all primary school life contributes to the development of these values and skills, it is now widely recognised that their attainment cannot be left to something as intangible and 'unexaminable' as the ethos of a school.

The understanding of concepts such as **what is fair**, or skills such as **moral and critical thinking**, develops most effectively as a result of carefully planned learning experiences. If this is left to chance, the children who most need to attain such skills and understanding may have the least opportunity to do so.

Much citizenship learning takes place concurrently as children learn to live and work together as members of the school group or community. The more children are encouraged to participate in community activities, the more likely they are to develop positive concerns about what happens in the wider world.

However, the role of a **citizen** is a demanding one. It requires specific knowledge and understanding of how people who are strangers to one another can engage in a shared public life based on a set of broadly agreed values, and can openly argue and work for change whilst respecting the right of others to oppose their views. Thus, a citizen must learn how to live both a private and a public life, alert to the creative tension between individual rights and 'the greater good'.

For children to internalise such complex social behaviour, a great deal of social learning and development is necessary. Education for citizenship occurs when such aims are prominent in teachers' planning and positively influence the nature of the teaching situation.

Teaching methods

Citizenship, like other areas of the curriculum, has its own language, core concepts and methods. In citizenship work we may ask questions about human needs or rights, or address wider issues about what it means to live together in harmony and justice. And since there are no single or simple answers to such questions, the controversial nature of citizenship becomes a focal part of the learning and profoundly influences the methods employed.

For this reason, much citizenship work is best undertaken as a communal activity, especially through the shared analysis of issues of common concern and group-based approaches to practical tasks. This is not only to learn the value of achieving a democratic consensus but also to emphasise the importance of reflection and consultation in making fair and wise decisions. It also underlines the value of pooling individual resources, skills and perspectives to achieve social change.

In various ways, teachers touch on such issues daily. However, the distinctive nature of citizenship as a curriculum subject or area of study has not had much close attention. There is still much to explore and understand through reflective practice and research.

KEY CONCEPTS OF CITIZENSHIP EDUCATION

The key concepts of citizenship are rights and responsibilities in relation to self, others and the wider community. Rights often clash with responsibilities and even with other rights. The need to reach a fair resolution of such conflicts introduces the third key concept of justice or fairness. Justice is a central value in public life not only because it is important to achieve political solutions which are fair to all parties but also because of the need to have procedures and institutions which can be seen by all citizens to be fair.

Triangle of key concepts

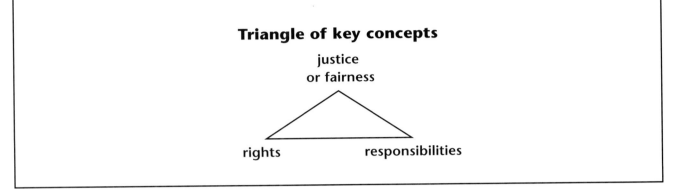

Citizenship issues will almost always be concerned with one or more of the above key concepts. They are also likely to touch on other ideas, such as:
• power and authority
• rules and laws
• democracy
• individual and community
• conflict and cooperation
• equality and difference.

When these concepts are applied to actual situations, even simple ones quite within the understanding of Key Stage 1 children, basic questions will arise in discussion. For example:

Rights
• What kinds of legal rights do people have?
• Should people have rights that they do not already have?
• Do any of these rights bring responsibilities with them?

Responsibilities
• What kinds of responsibilities or obligations do people have?
• Where do these responsibilities come from?
• Are the responsibilities fair?
• What should happen to people who ignore their responsibilities?

Justice
• Is this situation fair? Why? / Why not?
• What would make it fairer?

Power and authority
• Who in society has authority and why?
• How can people use their power or authority on behalf of others?
• Why do people misuse their power?
• What is the difference between proper use of authority and the improper use of power?

Rules and laws
• Why do we need rules?
• What is their function?
• What makes a rule a fair one?
• Who should have a say in deciding the rules?
• Which rules or laws would we like to change?
• Why can we do some things but are not allowed to do others?

Democracy

- What is democracy?
- Why is democracy thought to be a fair way of decision-making?
- How does one engage in democratic decision-making?
- Who makes our laws?
- How can our school be made more democratic?

Individual and community

- What is the link between individuals and the communities in which they live?
- In what ways can individuals contribute to their communities?
- What responsibilities does the community have towards its members?
- Why should people care about what goes on around them?
- How do society and social life work?
- Could things be better?

Conflict and cooperation

- What kinds of tensions exist between people in society and how can these be resolved?
- What benefits can be gained from cooperating with others?
- Can cooperating with others sometimes have disadvantages?
- When is compromise a good thing?
- When is compromise not a good thing?

Equality and difference

- In what ways should we regard and treat people as equals?
- When should we recognise and address the legitimate differences between people?

As well as these political, legal or social concepts, citizenship education concerns itself with concepts of **right and wrong**, and **good and bad**. It also encourages pupils to **respect** themselves and one another, and to care about what happens in the wider world. These concepts can be used to formulate questions in the same way.

LAYING THE FOUNDATIONS

The key concepts provide an essential guide to the way we think about moral and political issues. Even before children come to school, their understanding of concepts such as **fairness**, **power**, and **equality** are taking shape[1]. It is therefore important that schools are active in shaping their further development. Given the right conditions, these ideas will grow and develop as children mature.

> Research studies demonstrate that by the end of Key Stage 2, children have already accumulated a considerable awareness of society[2]. For example, many children can name the prime minister and have opinions about matters such as national government, the law, the police and the courts, racism and discrimination, even though these opinions are still only partially formed.

If it is accepted that citizenship learning is a developmental matter, then it becomes very important to recognise the significance of the primary years in laying the foundations for the more sophisticated learning that will take place in secondary school.

HOW DO CHILDREN LEARN CITIZENSHIP?

It is said that 'people only learn by doing', but actions of all kinds both express values and influence them. Children quickly learn to recognise when adults contradict their own words by their actions. Similarly, children's actions and experiences provide powerful learning experiences which involve both their heads and their emotions. The learning of citizenship values takes place through *thinking, feeling and doing*.

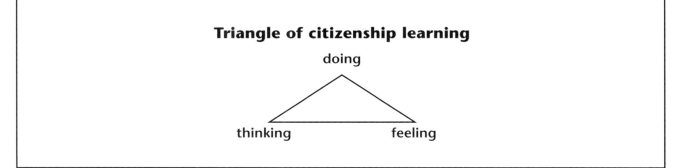

Triangle of citizenship learning

Thinking informs and, to some extent, controls the emotions, but feelings motivate us to care or not to care, to be involved or to withdraw. And both of these strongly influence our actions, the latter in turn shaping and developing how we think and feel. Citizenship education is a prime curriculum location for the promotion of emotional as well as moral and political literacy.

The non-statutory guidance for citizenship identifies the following three strands in citizenship education.

• Social and moral responsibility
• Community involvement
• Political literacy

This analysis emphasises that the teaching of citizenship involves something more significant and complex than imparting understanding of political ideas and knowledge of institutions. All three strands need to be present at each key stage, though with varying emphases according to age and ability. There is a close overlap with those aspects of the child's spiritual, moral, social and cultural development (SMSC) which it is part of the school's statutory duty to promote. The term SMSC was introduced to ensure the more holistic aims of education were not lost when the National Curriculum with its emphasis on knowledge accumulation was first introduced.

How does citizenship encourage SMSC?

All subject areas and the planned and unplanned experiences of school life contribute to spiritual, moral, social and cultural development. The following breakdown shows how each can be addressed through citizenship education.

Spiritual development

A school is a pluralistic community which provides an important forum for the discussion of ideas, beliefs and values of all kinds. In education, the term 'spiritual' is used in both a religious and secular sense to include children with no religious faith. Citizenship education helps to develop the spiritual dimension by promoting respect for individual beliefs and core values. It can help pupils explore the relationship between people's religious values and their social and political aspirations, as well as developing their ability and willingness to reflect on the meaning of life and how we should live.

When children discuss issues such as bullying, respect for property and responsibility to the environment, they bring their personal values into the forum of the classroom and learn what it takes to reach a common understanding and shared solutions in a manner essential to the democratic way of life.

Moral development

Citizenship education is centrally concerned with promoting moral thinking. Moral awareness helps children to develop a critical appreciation of issues of right and wrong, justice, fairness, and rights and obligations in society.

The child who acts in a truly moral way, is one who has internalised such values and can apply them in novel situations according to his or her own conscience. The process of internalisation takes time and effort. Citizenship education encourages it through reflection, debate and action. The internalisation of moral values is a vital aspect of citizenship education because without a personal moral sense there is little motivation to become involved in a community for the sake of other individuals or for the common good.

In so far as it is possible to say that public life is based on values such as honesty, reliability, concern for others and fairness, then promoting these moral values is an inescapable part of the teacher's task. However, the aim is not to try to promote a clear and unambiguous set of values for the children to follow without question. Even young children may already be experiencing conflicting values in their lives. For example, the difference between the values of their home and their school. In general, where issues are controversial in society, they should be acknowledged as such in the classroom.

Reasoning, perception and intuition all contribute to a child's moral thinking development. A significant amount of moral learning comes out of experience – 'actions speak louder than words'. If children are to develop moral values they need to be given opportunities to:

- reflect on and discuss the moral values embedded in familiar situations
- develop their ability to empathise with others
- recognise why moral conflicts arise and resolve them thoughtfully and with consideration for others

- take on responsibilities where possible
- learn from example and from positive relationships with adults
- understand that the values underpinning school life are consistent with those taught in the classroom.

Social development

Citizenship education encourages the individual to see him/herself as part of a wider community in which everyone matters and has a role to play. It highlights not only the rights of individuals but also their responsibilities to others, and encourages active participation in community affairs for the benefit of the common good. It is concerned with promoting knowledge about communities and how they are organised including civic, social, legal, economic and political aspects of how society functions. Such knowledge is essential if pupils are to become effective in public life.

The whole of school life contributes to the social education of children. Besides learning about the social world, they learn through experience what it means to be in different kinds of power relationship, about belonging to rule-governed communities, about pluralism and diversity, similarity and difference. Children's experiences (for example, of how adults use their power) contribute powerfully to what they learn about the way the world actually is, as opposed to how it is supposed to be.

Cultural development

Citizenship education promotes the child's cultural development by recognising that Britain is a multi-cultural society which has incorporated many of its current practices and values from other cultures. It promotes respect for pluralism, cultural diversity and difference based on notions of universal human rights. It also promotes respect for individual beliefs and customs.

THE DEVELOPMENT OF CHILDREN'S MORAL THINKING

Exploring moral issues in class and exposing children to more sophisticated thinking has been shown to accelerate the shift towards greater awareness and more mature moral thinking.

According to research[3], children in the primary years think in distinctive and recognisable ways about moral issues. The main characteristics of their thinking can be summarised as follows.

- It is concrete and egocentric.
- The motivation for good behaviour is often avoidance of punishment or other negative consequences; severe punishments are thought of as the best way to restrain the behaviour of others.
- Rules are more often thought of as boundaries to restrain behaviour, rather than positive principles for living.
- There is a relative lack of awareness of how others think and feel, leading to insensitive behaviour.
- Children have an 'external locus of control', i.e. children lack internal moral controls and look to authority figures, such as parents, teachers and police officers, to set rules and enforce behaviour. These internal controls tend to develop with a growing empathic awareness of others.

Under guidance from the teacher, classroom discussion of moral issues can move outwards from a child's immediate concerns towards those of others. Exploring other people's inner motivations and feelings helps children understand more than the external and the physical.

It is not enough for children to know that, for example, bullying and stealing are wrong. The question to ask is, 'why do you think such things are wrong?' If they believe it is wrong to bully others only because the teacher says so, or because they will get into trouble, there is nothing to stop them bullying when the teacher is not present. It is a sign of growing moral maturity when the child understands that bullying is intrinsically wrong because of the distress it causes the victim.

During the secondary years, wider social perspectives enter young people's thinking[2]. They might say bullying is wrong not only because of the effect it has on the victim but also because it undermines law and order. They may even refer to abstract principles such as human rights or non-violence. The following examples show how the attitudes that children have towards stealing progress from immature to mature thinking.

WHY IS IT WRONG TO STEAL?

Immature (egocentric)

It just is wrong.
You will get caught and put in prison.
Because if you steal from others, they might steal from you.
People will not like you if you are a thief.
Stealing is OK if you can get away with it or if everyone else does it.

Mature (other centred)

Concern for others

Stealing is wrong because it is unkind.

Stealing undermines trust between people or damages relationships.

It would hurt your parents' feelings if you were caught stealing.

Concern to uphold moral principles

If it's the law, it must be obeyed because that is what society has agreed.

Stealing harms communities and society needs order to avoid chaos.

Concern for society

Stealing simply is not honest and I believe that it is right to be as honest as possible in everything one does.

Ultimately stealing is wrong because it is a violation of people's rights to property. The law is only there to protect these rights.

2. THE IMPORTANCE OF TALK

PRACTICAL STRATEGIES FOR THE CLASSROOM

Through the medium of talk, we exchange ideas, come to understand ourselves and others better, reach shared understandings and determine joint courses of action. We also use talk to put forward minority opinions, to express disquiet, and to defend our rights or the rights of others. Talk is a fundamental medium through which we engage in citizenship activities.

If, through engagement with others, we develop more complex understandings of issues, or greater empathy with others, then democracy will be the stronger. Sometimes, it is harder to change one's own ideas than to do something physical. This is why it is so important that children learn to engage with one another at a personal level by expressing themselves through talk.

The encouragement of quality discussion and thinking is something to aspire to in all curriculum

areas, but citizenship issues offer particularly rich and stimulating opportunities for classroom discussion because children can draw on their own experiences, values and beliefs. The greater the children's involvement in an issue, the more likely they are to want to discuss it. This more committed engagement will lead to better quality talk and the greater possibility of intellectual growth.

Classes with a strong sense of community are more likely to enjoy good quality talk. And the better the quality of the talk in class, the greater the possibility of a strong sense of community. The discussion of moral issues requires an atmosphere of trust and understanding which can only be developed over time. It needs to be worked at patiently and systematically.

If issues such as stealing or bullying are discussed only in a crisis, an atmosphere of blame or inquisition could inhibit calm enquiry. It can be more helpful to create a climate in which the children regularly talk about difficult issues. This will develop sensitivities and techniques which can be drawn on when a crisis does occur. The teacher will then be able to refer to ideas already discussed and utilise the trust and understanding already built up within the group.

Many factors contribute to the way in which children explore issues together. Some relate to the physical environment, including how the children are seated, but more have to do with the way in which learning tasks are structured by the teacher. The following strategies have all been found to be effective and may be used at different times to facilitate different types of discussion. Many of them are demonstrated on the accompanying video.

Getting started

You may wish to timetable a discussion each week. Alternatively, you could use closely linked blocks over shorter periods of time, for example, by exploring one issue during a short session every day for a week. This is often helpful in the early days of developing discussion skills.

Like everything else, training is necessary to establish the ground rules and the children's expectations, so regularity is valuable. Discussion work links well with Literacy Hour and Circle Time activities. Don't give up if things don't work out well the first time. It may take a few sessions to establish group expectations and for you to begin to see the benefits.

ESTABLISH GROUND RULES

A few ground rules for discussion work must be established from the outset. It is very important that the children are involved in making the rules. In most cases, children come up with roughly similar sets of rules. The last two rules (above right) may not come from the children themselves but they are important for developing reasoning as a

collective activity. You may like to introduce them as your contribution for discussion and acceptance by the group. When the children have agreed on the rules, they should be written out and displayed as a reminder to the group. At the end of each session, the children can review their list of rules and discuss whether or not they want to revise or add to them.

Rules for a Citizenship Circle

- Only one person talks at a time.
- Listen carefully and don't distract each other.
- Respect what others have to say.
- It's OK to disagree.
- Always be prepared to give a reason for your opinion.
- Try to 'follow on' from what has just been said.

USE EXPLORATORY TALK TO ENCOURAGE CRITICAL THINKING

Critical thinking is a term often used but less often defined. In the context of a citizenship class, critical thinking may involve children in:

- expressing opinions which are genuinely their own and not merely repeating what they feel they should say
- examining different sides of an issue in order to improve understanding
- offering new insights or perspectives
- challenging the views of others, including the teacher's
- applying moral principles to real contexts or new situations
- accepting the views of others, after consideration (changing their minds)
- justifying a view with evidence
- speculating or hypothesising.

Questions from the children

Encouraging the children to ask questions is a good way to support critical thinking, but children often find this difficult when they are not used to it. Their questioning skills can be greatly improved with encouragement and practice.

After reading a story with the children, ask them to suggest some questions about it that they would like to discuss in class. List the questions and ask them to vote on which ones they would like to examine and in what order. It may not be appropriate to use this method all the time, but it does quickly help the children to realise that almost any topic or action can be subject to critical enquiry. The process of framing and selecting questions gives the class a sense of ownership of the lesson, which can help to motivate them. Pupils benefit from being given models of questions. Alternatively, you could give them the words **who**, **what**, **where**, **when**, **how** and **why**, and encourage them to ask a partner questions using each of these initial words.

Questions from the teacher

Carefully chosen questions can be genuinely stimulating and encourage exploratory talk, but research has shown they can also have the opposite effect and stifle originality. If open discussion is to flourish, the well established technique of asking leading questions needs to be 'unlearned', and this can take time and effort.

General questions to improve children's understanding and enrich discussion	
Aim	Question
To direct the children's thinking towards a specific issue.	What do you think about [...]?
To find out the children's concerns.	Is there anything in the story that you would like to talk about?
To discover the children's perceptions.	What do you think of that?
To assess the children's understanding of a word or concept.	What do you think that means?
To encourage the children to examine or justify an opinion.	Why do you think that?
To encourage the children to clarify their statements.	What do you mean by that?
To assess whether there is a consensus.	Who agrees with this?
To encourage the children to make judgements.	Do you think that is fair?
To encourage pupils to predict outcomes.	What do you think will happen next?
To develop imagination.	What would you do if [...]?
To encourage negotiation.	Can you agree on [what choice of action is best]?
To recap or sum up.	What have we thought about so far?

Questions to promote moral awareness	
Aim	Question
To develop empathy.	Who do you feel most sorry for in the story? ... Why? What are the needs of the person in the story? How do you think s/he was feeling?
To focus thinking on the justice of a situation.	Do you think that is fair? ... Why? / Why not?
To consider moral actions or principles.	Was that a good or bad thing to do? ... Why?
To examine a person's motives or intentions.	Why do you think s/he did that?
To examine the rights implicit in a situation.	Do you think s/he had a right to do that? ... Why? / Why not?
To consider what obligations or duties a person might have.	What should s/he have done in that situation?
To examine possible consequences.	What would happen if they acted in this way?
To make a connection with the children's own experience.	Has anything like that happened to you? ... What did you do? ... Why?
To encourage expression of feelings.	How did you feel about that?

Getting the children to talk

While questions are essential to stimulate discussion, they should be used judiciously. Research[1] has shown that the more questions teachers ask, the less children talk. Therefore, better quality discussion is likely to develop when teachers:
• talk less
• ask fewer but more open questions
• share in the enquiry with the children, modelling reflective thinking
• avoid commenting on what a child says; but instead, offer it to the group to respond
• give the children more time to think, pausing longer between questions.

It is not enough to ask the questions and listen to the responses. This in itself will not necessarily move the children forward in their moral reasoning. The initial question should be seen as the beginning of a mini-discussion in which the teacher supports the children's thinking by offering the question for examination by the group, clarifying responses, correcting mis-information, asking for other points of view and so on. The teacher may then sum up the children's responses and move their thinking into new areas, or follow the children's own line of enquiry.

PROGRESSION IN CHILDREN'S TALK

In a study of children working in small discussion groups, Neil Mercer[2] observed that children tend to adopt three different modes of talk. He observed that the more crude forms of discourse, which he called 'disputational' and 'cumulative' talk, given the right conditions will gradually give way to more sophisticated 'exploratory' talk.

Disputational talk (uncooperative)

Younger children tend to make isolated statements, at first showing little ability to engage with what others are saying. Older children can also display an inability to engage constructively with others. They argue their case by simple assertion of their position, offering no justification and possibly using ridicule or other 'put-downs' to win an argument.

Cumulative talk (cooperative but non-critical)

A simple form of engagement with the ideas of others is to use them uncritically by repeating the idea or adding to it. Some children immediately modify their own position to comply with the statements of others.

Exploratory talk

This is the most sophisticated form of talk and takes time to learn. In exploratory talk, Mercer suggests:

... partners engage critically but constructively with each other's ideas... statements and suggestions are offered for joint consideration. These may be challenged and counter-challenged, but challenges are justified and alternative hypotheses offered. Compared with the other two types, in exploratory talk knowledge is made more publicly accountable and reasoning is more visible in the talk.

Mercer's research found that improvements in the quality of exploratory talk help children to reason more effectively, increasing their understanding of key concepts. Also, intervention by the teacher through practice sessions of structured talk can increase children's use of exploratory talk and raise their scores in reasoning tests.

WHAT TO TALK ABOUT

Talking about an issue, whether real or fictional, allows children to draw
on and extend their own world view. Stories, therefore, are particularly
valuable as starting points for the exploration of a wide range of
citizenship issues. Their use is dealt with in detail in Chapter 3.
Below are some of the many other stimuli that can be used
to spark off good quality talk.

Pupils' own ideas

Any topic which encompasses citizenship issues is suitable for discussion. Topics may well come from the pupils' own concerns and interests once they begin to recognise the value of sharing them in discussion. At intervals through a term, allocate time to discuss the children's topics. Flagging this in advance will give them time to come up with ideas.

Invite the children to suggest topics for discussion. Make and display a list of their ideas so it can be added to over the days before the discussion. They can then vote for the topic they want to talk about.

Sometimes, older children might want to discuss an incident in the news which they have found bewildering or disturbing. The forum of a class discussion will allow them to express their concerns or confusion and can help them to make sense of what has happened. At the same time, it confirms to the children that their concerns are recognised as valid.

Issues arising from the life of the school

Issues that arise within the school or class often provide valuable opportunities to involve pupils in class decisions. These can range from deciding on the class rules, to working out how to deal with issues such as bullying and litter in the school. This community approach to problem-solving not only allows a more complex and realistic picture to develop, it also emphasises that such problems can only be solved with everyone's help.

The news[3] and current affairs

Many children are not aware of what is happening in the wider world. They may not watch children's news programmes or ever see a newspaper. Children in Key Stage 2 should increasingly be encouraged to look at newspapers for articles to bring to school for class debate. The children's suggestions can be listed and voted on for discussion by the whole class. Initially, you may need to model this around an article you have chosen. It is useful to offer initial guidelines to frame the discussion and aid understanding.
For example:

• What/who is the story about?
• Why do you think this might have happened?
• Who was responsible?
• What are the likely consequences?
• Is the newspaper version likely to be reliable?

Apart from the current issues covered in news items, there are many contemporary themes to which children can relate. Themes which could be explored in a number of different ways include:
• multiracial awareness
• rights of minority groups
• personal relationships
• improving the local community
• caring for the environment
• the role of the police and other public services
• crime and punishment
• similarities and differences between people, behaviours, cultures or groups
• people in distant places and times
• living together
• what people believe
• conflict and cooperation.

Television

Soap operas and other television programmes watched by the majority of children can be a rich source of material for exploring issues relating to community life. It has been argued that it is through television that many children receive much of their knowledge of how society operates.

It is important to monitor the messages being conveyed because some children can confuse fiction with reality. Such monitoring is best done through discussion and exploring the reality of situations shown on television.

Fruitful talk can come out of looking at certain characters in soap operas and exploring their motives and the consequences of their actions. Ask pupils to identify which character they would most want to be like and why. This can be a good starting point for discussion on how people interact in the community.

As parents differ widely in what they wish their children to watch, care is needed to ensure that children from homes where television viewing is more circumscribed are not excluded from such discussions. This can be avoided by giving a quick summary of the plot, characters and action at the beginning of the discussion.

Drama and role play

A wide range of issues can be explored through role play and drama. Small groups of children could act out situations which can then be discussed by the whole group. Allow each child to decide which role they want to play. It can be useful to make a set of situation cards which include both positive and negative situations. The *Thinkers* picture books, as well as many other story books, can provide ideas for role play situations. Acting out the stories helps children to understand more about the issues and emotions involved.

Good examples include the roles of Stanley and Zero from *Holes* by Louis Sachar (Bloomsbury). The boys escape from a juvenile detention centre where their 'character building' punishment has been to dig holes in an arid lake bed. Stanley was innocent. Zero was guilty but has no parents, can't read, and has had to steal to survive for as long as he can remember. Thrown together in a desert prison, they learn to trust and depend on one another. This simply written story will stimulate lively discussions of issues that will take in the core concepts of justice and fairness, rights and responsibility, as well as authority, power, bullying, friendship, loyalty, trust, the value of families and the consequences of past events.

Pictures

With all children, particularly younger ones or where language difficulties are present, pictures can be a great impetus for discussion. A whole range of images can be used, such as magazine pictures, paintings and the children's own drawings. One advantage offered by pictures is that children draw directly on their own experience or world view in interpreting them. This can be extremely valuable in detecting the orientation of their concerns. You can start the discussion by asking questions such as:

- What do you think is happening in this picture?
- Is there anything in the picture that you would like to talk about?
- What would you like to know about the people or what they are doing?

Visitors

An important element of citizenship education is involvement in the wider community. Visitors from organisations, such as the police, fire service, hospital or a local charity, could be invited into school to talk about their work and to answer questions prepared by the children. Such visits help pupils understand how certain organisations work. Groups of older children could invite local councillors or other community leaders to provide expert information, preferably in relation to a specific issue, rather than for a generalised talk about, say, the role of local government.

Information Technology

The Internet now provides a huge range of opportunities for citizenship education. It is possible to establish conferences on selected topics between a number of schools. Children in different countries can exchange information about their values and beliefs via the Internet.

WHERE TO TALK

There are many ways of organising the children, whether you are working with the whole class at once or with small groups of children. Choose a seating arrangement that suits the kind of discussion you are aiming to generate.

Carpet group

Whole group sessions with younger children sitting on the carpet facing you can work well. They provide good opportunities for the children to listen to a story and for the teacher to elicit from them how well they have understood it. The children's proximity to the teacher can create a sense of togetherness and help younger children to be heard by all the other children.

However, this arrangement can inhibit children from engaging with each other because their attention is focused on the teacher. Since they see few other faces, discussion almost inevitably goes back and forth between teacher and children like a ball between tennis players. Furthermore, exchanges between the teacher and children at the front can exclude those further back. Carpet groups seem better suited to situations where the flow of talk is mainly from teacher to children.

Grouped at tables

With older children, a good way to start is with the teacher talking from the front with the children sitting at their tables, but it is important to encourage the children to look at whoever is speaking. After this they can split into table groups for further discussion. Table groups are probably not a sensible arrangement for an extended or whole-class discussion. They can work well enough where groups take it in turn to feed back the results of their discussion but extended feedback sessions are difficult to sustain. As with carpet groups, children can become excluded if they cannot hear what is being said by children across the room.

Seated in a circle

Sitting at the same level as the children in a circle can provide the best arrangement for discussions in which all children are expected to engage. Eye contact can be maintained and facial expressions seen, which add life and feeling to what is said. Also, being able to see lip movements can aid hearing. Another advantage is that everyone, including the teacher, is physically equal within the circle. Seated in this way, children are more likely to address each other rather than addressing their comments solely to the teacher. The circle arrangement can also make it easy to break up a whole group discussion into smaller buzz groups of two or three children, before coming back together again.

If the room is not large enough for a circle to be arranged away from the tables, it may be possible to bunch them together and make a larger circle around them. Moving the children from the middle to the outside can be done quickly and easily. Establishing a set routine, so that the children know exactly which chairs or tables they each need to move to achieve the new arrangement, will speed up the process.

Circle Time routines, such as going round the circle completing a sentence stem, can establish from the outset that everyone's contribution is important. This type of exercise can also support quiet children and help them to overcome their inhibitions. Children who do not want to speak need to be allowed to 'pass', but it helps to make it clear that a contribution will be just as welcome from them later when they have had a little more thinking time.

> ### Some stem questions for citizenship work
>
> - I think [sharing] is good because...
> - I think it's wrong to [steal] because...
> - I felt most sorry for [...] because...
> - If I were [...] I would have...
> - That [kind of behaviour] makes me feel...

Half class groups

The size of an average class undoubtedly makes it more difficult to have meaningful discussions in which all children engage equally. Even for adults, groups of thirty can be inhibiting and tend not to involve the participants at an optimum level. Larger groups favour the more articulate and confident child and this can make it difficult to monitor the extent to which all children are participating. Going around the circle even on one issue can take quite a long time and loss of concentration may occur after a child's turn has passed. Working with only half the class at a time can work well and generate more in-depth discussion.

One discussion group

It may be possible for half the class to work with a classroom assistant somewhere else (for example, in the library) during discussion time. Alternatively, you could set work for one group, training them not to interrupt, whilst you conduct a discussion with the remainder. However, this would require a large classroom and the quiet working group may find it difficult not to be distracted by the discussion. A classroom assistant or parent helper could oversee the 'quiet working group'.

Two discussion groups

Another option is to split the class into two equal discussion groups and have a student teacher, nursery nurse or classroom assistant lead one of them. This can work very well if the less experienced group leader is given some training in group facilitation and on how to support open discussion. It would also help if the first one or two sessions are shared.

Smaller groups

Some topics lend themselves to discussion in small groups prior to a whole class forum. The advantage of this is that every child should be able to come to the circle with something they have already thought about. Consideration needs to be given to the size of the small group in relation to the age of the children. Paired discussion is a valuable way of getting children tuned in to particular aspects of an issue.

It is a good idea to introduce a topic to the whole class, then to divide the children into small table groups, each with a question to discuss. Circulate amongst the groups giving additional questions and re-directing where needed. The questions can be written out on cards for the children to refer to. Any additional adult can help to keep groups on-task. The main points can be brought out and discussed further in a plenary session.

At first, children may feel most at ease discussing a topic among children with whom they usually work. It is then worth varying the composition of the groups to encourage social mixing. Each child will benefit from the opportunity to discuss issues with children who come from a wide variety of backgrounds. This supports the idea that talking is a serious activity and can be much more than a casual chat with friends.

It is worth remembering that many children who experience difficulty with reading and writing have highly developed discussion skills. You may also wish to change the groups depending on the topic being discussed.

CHOOSING HOW TO GROUP THE CHILDREN

It is useful to experiment with different groupings as the dynamics created by different combinations of children can greatly affect the quality of discussion. One piece of research into grouping[4] found that:

- grouping the extroverts together stopped them dominating other groups, yet enabled each to express their opinion.
- grouping quieter children together worked well. They felt less intimidated and were more able to share ideas within a like-minded group. These children produced thoughtful ideas, which they had not done when in mixed groups.
- less able children benefited from working with more able children.

3. Literacy and Citizenship

Using Stories and Language to Prompt Discussion

A great deal of children's thinking energy goes into trying to make sense of the world around them. In their book, *Young Children Learning: talking and thinking at home and at school*, Tizard and Hughes[1] reported on the interactions of 30 four-year-old girls with their mothers. They noted that the children often became fascinated or absorbed with an idea and struggled to understand it through questioning and internal thought. Subjects included things such as: why roofs slope, what money is for, and the nature of Father Christmas. Sometimes, the children would puzzle away for a long time, returning again and again in conversation to the same theme until they were satisfied or eventually gave up. Tizard and

Hughes called these episodes 'passages of intellectual search'.

Sadly, the study found that these young children mostly confined such episodes of curiosity to when they were at home. At school, they quickly learnt who dictates the learning agenda.

Part of what citizenship education is about is to promote the conditions in which children can feel empowered to undertake **jointly** passages of intellectual search around social and moral issues. One very effective way to stimulate such enquiry-based learning is to use stories as a basis for joint reflection.

THE VALUE OF EXPLORING STORIES

Stories can provide the kind of rich stimulus that a child is able to approach from a personal viewpoint. Stories are capable of taking us beneath the surface events of life to reveal motives and feelings. Very much according to their own experience and way of thinking, different readers will impute different motives to the characters. They will sympathise with the same kinds of people in a story as they would do in real life. By discussing a story, or other piece of narrative, children can bring their own understanding and concerns to the class and set them alongside those of other children. Some children will bring a more complex or sophisticated understanding of the narrative to the discussion and this will enrich, even transform, the way others interpret the story.

Stories convey much that cannot easily be put into words; a few simple phrases can encapsulate many layers of meaning for children. **Actions** can be deconstructed in terms of **motives**, **feelings**, **hopes** or **fears**; while **abstract ideas**, such as **fairness** or **honesty**, can be dealt with in considerable complexity when approached via a narrative.

Citizenship issues are a complex mix of **action**, **beliefs** and **values**, involving individuals in relation to others and the wider community, and stories often contain the problematic dynamics of such inter-relationships. Exploring and talking about such fictional relationships helps children to understand some of the complexities of how they and other people relate to one another and work together in communities.

Furthermore, working with stories can be an invaluable way of examining the difficulties of living in a moral way. For example, the characters in a story may be torn between conflicting responsibilities, not knowing which way to choose for the best.

The narrative can act as a kind of mirror for readers, perhaps allowing them to recognise things about themselves. For example, on the video, one of the Year 1 children discussing *The Sand Tray* is able, without prompting, to recognise something of his own selfishness through the description of Johnny's behaviour. In joint reflection of such a narrative, children can move on to learn the shared language of moral analysis and explore the issues in far greater depth than they could do on their own.

However, it can never be assumed that this process will take place automatically. If children do not engage personally with a narrative, then no genuine reflection will take place. This is why it is so valuable to engage their emotions as well as their intellect – something that stories can do supremely well.

Generating discussion

Many, if not most, stories can be used for citizenship work, although some are far richer in texture than others and give the children more to work with. Stories are often so rich that only a few of the questions they raise can be pursued satisfactorily during any one session. It is very helpful for teachers if they talk to one another about the stories that have provoked thoughtful responses from the children and what particular issues different stories can access.

At the back of each *Thinkers* picture book there are some starter questions relating to the story. It is not intended that the suggested questions be used slavishly. That would be to disregard the unique way in which any discussion develops. The discussion needs to follow the interests of the class whilst not wandering too far from the central points. With encouragement and as they grow in confidence the children will soon be generating questions of their own.

Before introducing your own questions, it is valuable to first ask the children if there is anything they would like to discuss. Whilst flexibility about what is discussed is important, it is a good idea to make a note of the content of each discussion so as to ensure that different types of questions are covered regularly, especially those that develop **empathy**, **moral reasoning** and **critical enquiry** and allow the children to draw on their own experiences.

Ask the children questions such as:

- Why do you think the person in the story did that?
- Was that right, in your opinion?
- Was there something else they could have done?

Such questions are valuable because they require children to **make judgements** rather than merely give a comprehension-type answer.

To help the children arrive at a better, more informed, understanding of each situation, the next step is to look at the range of different judgements made during their discussions and compare them in the light of available evidence.

Questions may emerge as the story unfolds (as seen in Section 3 of the video); or they can focus on the main issues that come out of the story as a whole. Be clear at the outset which you would prefer, because it affects whether the story is read right through in one session or read section by section. There is a lot to be said for reading the story twice, since much more can be drawn from the story when the context of the events is better understood and the children's attention is less focused on the surface events of the plot. Some stories bear repeated readings, each time looking at a different theme.

THINKERS PICTURE BOOKS

The *Thinkers* stories provide a starting point for the discussion of a variety of issues.

Title	Key Issues
JOE'S CAR Annabelle Dixon and Tim Archbold	Respect for property, sharing, honesty, forgiveness
THE SAND TRAY Don Rowe and Tim Archbold	Rules, rights, responsibilities, authority, friendship, fairness, loyalty
THE SCARY VIDEO Gill Rose and Tim Archbold	Television-viewing, fear, responsibility
WILLIAM AND THE GUINEA-PIG Gill Rose and Tim Archbold	Responsibility, caring for other creatures, family, forgiveness

OTHER STORIES FOR THINKING

In addition to books conceived specifically to provide 'stories for thinking', many hundreds of other story books touch on ideas and themes of importance to the lives of children and young people. Teachers will have their own favourites and every school library will have a good stock of possibilities to explore. Here, together with some of the main issues they address, are just a few of the many titles we could recommend.

Ages	Title	Key Issues
5–8	JIM AND THE BEANSTALK Raymond Briggs Picture Puffin	Fear and size
	ROSIE SIPS SPIDERS Alison Lester Oxford University Press	Respecting others
5–10	WILLY THE CHAMP WILLY THE WIMP Anthony Browne Walker Books	Bullying
	SNOW WOMAN David McKee Andersen Press (hb) Red Fox (pb)	Gender issues
	TUSK, TUSK David McKee Andersen Press (hb) Red Fox (pb)	Prejudice, intolerance, war and peace
6–8	BUT MARTIN June Counsel Faber & Faber (hb) Picture Corgi (pb)	Respect for other cultures
6–11	HURRAH FOR ETHELYN Babette Cole Heinemann (hb) Mammoth (pb)	Ganging up, name calling
7–11	I'LL TAKE YOU TO MRS COLE Nigel Gray Andersen Press	Parenthood, threats
8+	THE MAN WHOSE MOTHER WAS A PIRATE Margaret Mahy Puffin	Stereotyping
8–11	COMING ROUND[2] Antony Lishak	Breaking the law, helping others, loyalty, 'telling tales'

DISCUSSION IN THE LITERACY HOUR

Mark Prentice (see video, Section 3), now a head teacher, has spent many years working on an approach to the development of thinking, speaking and listening through the use of story books. His scheme, outlined below, fits well into the recommendations for literacy work and accords with the government's support for the development of critical thinking across the curriculum.

Thinking and talking together

The aim of the scheme is to develop the children's **speaking and listening skills**. It also increases their skills of **inference and deduction** when studying literary texts. It is particularly rewarding to see children changing their minds and modifying their opinions as a result of discussion. It is also rewarding when something a child has said is challenged and they go on to reconsider and clarify what they originally thought in order to justify it. Sometimes, a discussion will usefully throw up a question that the children can only answer by going away to seek information from other sources and perhaps bringing this to the next session.

Generally, one story or picture book is explored for half a term because it is important that children **take time to discuss the issues** arising from a text rather than racing through the story. The **role of the teacher is crucial** in giving depth to the children's dialogue. It is necessary for teachers to be flexible in their own thinking, while watching out for and reacting to issues and interpretations raised by the children. At the same time, the teacher is responsible for encouraging and maintaining the **philosophical, enquiring, analytic nature** of the dialogue.

It helps to think of discussions as having, potentially, five stages. While the stages need not follow one another in strict sequence, they do represent a deepening of the level of discussion, a movement from the specific and the concrete towards the more general or abstract. The following five-stage model helps in the framing of questions that will suit the level of discussion in which the children are involved at any particular time.

Stage 1 Introduction and recapitulation

Remind the children of what has happened in the story so far and what was discussed during the previous week's session. This is the time for **justifying and elaborating** on the class's developing interpretations of the unfolding story.

Often, children's thinking will have moved on during the intervening week, so it is helpful to start a session by asking:

- Has anyone changed their mind or modified their opinion about anything they thought or said last time?
- Does anyone want to add to anything they said in a previous session?

Read the new section or chapter of the story to the whole class. Another option is to alternate the reading between the teacher and the children, or to ask the children to read the dialogue parts of different characters in the story.

Stage 2 Issues relevant to a particular story

Discuss questions relating to the plot. For example:

- What happened first in the story? ... Then what happened? ... Why?
- Did you guess what was going to happen in the end? ... If not, what did you think was going to happen?
- What would happen if the order of events was changed in the story?
- Can you think of a different ending to the story? ... How would the rest of the story have to be changed?
- When did the story take place? What makes you think that?
- Where do you think the story happens?
- Which character did you like the most/least? ... Why?
- Why do you think the characters behaved as they did?
- Do you know any people like the characters in the book?
- How do you think [...] felt when [...]?
- Did any of the characters change their behaviour during the course of the story? ... Why do you think that happened?

As well as looking for meaning within the text, encourage the children to look for visual clues in the pictures. Ask them to justify their views and to compare them with the interpretations of others. Challenge the children's assumptions, perhaps by asking them how they arrived at a particular interpretation:

- What made you think that?
- How do you know what you said is true or relevant?

If this is the first session with a story, start by examining the front cover picture in this way.

Stage 3 Key themes and philosophical or moral issues

Themes and issues arise naturally during a group's joint consideration of a story and are often related to children's own lives. In this stage, try to help them use their shared experience of reading the story to make connections with broader issues. The sharing of different perspectives on the issues is a crucial element. As with other areas of focus, pupils need to justify their opinions, using the text and their own experiences to support a statement.

Examples of broader issues might include:

- When are secrets good and when are they bad?
- How can we tell if people are unhappy?
- Is it right to lie about how you are feeling?
- What sort of things make friends fall out with one another?
- Does the author use stereotypes of gender, race, age, colour?

Stage 4 Reflections on the text and the process of reading

Pupils need to consider the literary style of the text by studying sections of a chapter. Discussion should focus on the writer's choice of **words and phrases**, the use of **figurative language** to create a mood or atmosphere, **recurring themes, symbols and imagery** and the **point of view** adopted by the story. For example:

- How would this chapter be different if it were written from another character's point of view?
- Who was telling the story?
- Were there any parts you particularly liked or disliked? ... Why?
- Who do you think the book is written for? ... Someone older/younger?

Stage 5 Reflections on the session so far

It is important to set aside some time before the end of each session to recap on the issues raised, to decide what needs to be focused on next time, and also to reflect on the class's performance in discussion. Ask questions such as:

- What have we discussed today?
- Has this session clarified our ideas about [...]?
- Have more of us talked this week?
- What shall we discuss next week?
- Are we getting better at finding clues?
- In what ways are we getting better at reading?

Plan your sessions to include some time, when the whole book is finished, to consider it as a whole by drawing on the same categories of question as appropriate.

THE VALUE OF 'TOOL WORDS'

Citizenship education in the primary school frequently uses words such as **fairness, rights** and **respect**. It is all too easy to assume children have a reasonable understanding of such terms and that each one has a **common meaning** to all children. However, an oral or written investigation in any classroom will demonstrate that the **same word** is likely to **mean something different** to each of the children and their responses are likely to show a wide range of misunderstandings.

Children frequently mis-hear or misunderstand the key words and this can frustrate the original intentions of citizenship education. We may smile at children's howlers, such as 'panda meat' for 'pound of meat', but any such misunderstanding should be taken seriously as it reveals where the children really are in their thinking.

Simply telling children what certain words **mean** is not enough and can lead to them recognising the sound of a word without understanding its actual meaning. Involving the whole class in a proactive and structured exploration of the meaning of key or **tool** words prepares the ground for citizenship education. It can also form part of the actual basis of the curriculum, especially in the early years. This

kind of involvement gives children access to language they can use as a genuine means of communication and thought.

Without such exploration into the **meaning of words** many children will merely acquire a superficially understood vocabulary that has little real meaning for them.

Understanding the tool words helps children to think clearly and communicate more easily with one another and with adults. If the children know, and have **made sense** of, the basic tool words and phrases at a personal level, they will be able to use them more effectively in class discussions and rely on the other children knowing what they mean.

Debating is one of the key skills in the curriculum for citizenship education, and the process of exploring the meaning of words with the rest of the class clearly deepens children's understanding. One way of assessing the benefits is to notice how the key words of citizenship education become a 'meaning-full' part of the children's own vocabulary, not just in the conversations they have with adults but also among the children themselves.

Exploring meaning

To explore the meaning of words as used in education for citizenship at the primary stage, it is necessary to establish some key or **tool** words. In practice, teachers have found the following words to be some of the most useful: **change**, **compare**, **different**, **opposite**, **similar**, **identical**, **set**, **problem**, **solve** and **question**. Others deal with feelings, such as: **disappointed**, **proud**, **glad** and so on.

At first glance these tool words may not seem specifically relevant to citizenship education but working with them does help even the younger children to frame their arguments more thoughtfully, to pose questions, and to articulate their opinions more clearly. They can be particularly helpful to children who, lacking the language skills to explain themselves coherently, tend to resort to aggression when faced with a problem.

Other words and phrases particularly relevant to citizenship education at the primary stage include: **respect**, **point of view**, **imagination**, **teamwork**, **decision**, **agree/disagree**, **fairness**, **friendship**, **rights** and **responsibilities**. Words such as **good/bad**, **kind/unkind** also have their place and confirm the close connection and overlap of citizenship with moral education.

This approach to the **exploration of meaning** needs to be flexible so that teachers can include and emphasise other words, according to their own experience and insight into the particular needs of their school, class or children. The principle aim is to give children a **mutually understood language** in which to think critically and to communicate about issues which are of concern to them and relevant to their communities.

Teachers will have their own way of introducing various words to the class. Together with the choice of words, it will be influenced by the background and abilities of the children. At the primary school stage of intellectual and moral development, children will have ideas and opinions that cannot be expected to be 'adult'. But as they become more articulate in thought and conversation, they develop the skills necessary to debate citizenship issues without being held back by a lack of an appropriate language.

AGREEING ON MEANING

To be effective, the introduction of tool words needs to be based on the principle that the children first agree on _jointly negotiated meanings_ for them. The following example of teaching practice demonstrates the benefits of such an approach.

A class of six-year-olds were introduced by their teacher to the word **respect**. She read them a story in which respect was an important component and briefly discussed with the children what it meant.

She then used the concept of opposites to help the children clarify their understanding. She asked them to think of instances of behaviour which, in their opinion, demonstrated either respect or disrespect, and to bring their examples to discussion times over the forthcoming week. The examples were to be written up on a large sheet of paper under one of two headings, **respect** and **disrespect** – but only, and this was the critical point, **after** the class had discussed them and agreed where they should be included.

The children were already familiar with discussion times and had learnt the ground rules about speaking in turn and how to agree and disagree in a non-aggressive manner. The teacher acted as manager and helped the less articulate but was not the final arbiter. The examples they agreed on included:

- 'My friend does not respect my brains when he talks to me while I'm trying to work.'
- 'It is not respecting yourself to swear at yourself.'

These examples reflected the lives and pre-occupations of the children but also helped to lay the groundwork for understanding a concept basic to citizenship education.

Having understood this way of learning the meaning of new words, the class became enthusiastic participators and started using the words amongst themselves, including when trying to solve real life arguments. When they subsequently debated the inclusion of new examples, their reasoning had demonstrably improved. Since the children drew on their own life experiences, the words were of particular relevance and importance to them; and they soon started to recognise examples of the various behaviours or concepts in stories. For example, following an argument between two fictional characters, one of the children commented:

- 'If they'd known how to **agree** and **disagree** they wouldn't have fallen out and they'd still be friends, wouldn't they, Miss?'

4. WHOLE SCHOOL ISSUES

CITIZENSHIP IN DAILY SCHOOL LIFE

Learning what it means to be an active and participating citizen is not confined to lesson time; it goes on throughout a child's whole school life. We need to be aware of the messages children pick up from everything they experience in school. And the **messages need to be consistent**. For example, if children are encouraged to believe they have the right to respect and to be free from discrimination, then their school experiences should underline rather than undermine that message.

There is, therefore, a need to identify precisely which school experiences have an impact on children's citizenship learning. Here, as with curriculum and lesson planning, the key citizenship concepts can be very useful since pupils' ideas about these concepts are powerfully influenced by their experiences as well as by what they learn in class. Think, for example, about how and where in school children learn about the nature of **fairness, rights, responsibilities, power, authority, equality, community, democracy, conflict** and **cooperation**. These will be crucial areas to examine in undertaking a whole school audit and policy review. For example, their beliefs about the real nature of power and authority will be influenced by what they see in the way teachers conduct themselves, relate to children and non-teaching staff, show respect, enforce rules fairly, show kindness and understanding, treat children as individuals, and so on. Also, children will learn about democracy and their rights to be heard if class and school rules are open to constructive criticism, and if children are invited to contribute to the running of the school as significant members of it.

ESTABLISHING A WHOLE SCHOOL APPROACH

Four areas of school life are relevant to developing a whole school approach towards citizenship: curriculum, policy, school ethos, and matters relating to the wider community, including relations with parents.

Consider the following questions.

Curriculum

 Does the school curriculum provide sufficient opportunity for the development of **knowledge and understanding** at the same time as developing **skills of enquiry and communication** and **participation**?

Does the curriculum specifically allow opportunities to encourage **positive values**, such as respect for diversity? Are these opportunities planned and reinforced for all pupils as an entitlement?

By the end of Key Stage 2, will the children have had an opportunity to consider **local, national and global** aspects of citizenship (for example, by learning about the lives of those in other countries and about our global environmental responsibilities)?

Are there clear, strong **links** between citizenship and other work, including RE, Literacy Hour, Speaking and Listening, and Circle Time, so that each reinforces the other? Are opportunities taken to overlap work and maximise the coverage of citizenship issues?

Does the curriculum provide for **continuity and progression**, such that **skills and concepts** introduced at Key Stage 1 are **revisited** later on? Are the children presented with greater challenges as they get older?

 Are all members of staff aware of the **range of resources** which can be used for citizenship work? For example, is there a recommended list of useful library books which focus on citizenship themes?

Policy

Does the **overall policy framework** for the school take account of the fact that education for citizenship is seen as a fundamental aim of education, as set out in the Statement of Values for Curriculum 2000?

 Does the school's **behaviour policy** demonstrate commitment to values of fairness and reasonableness? Are all children's rights properly safeguarded by disciplinary procedures? Are children given opportunities to take responsibility for their own actions? When children break the school rules, are they given opportunities to reflect on their behaviour, make amends or otherwise learn positively from the experience?

☐ Does the school do all it can to **ensure equality of access** to learning for all its pupils?

☐ Is the school a 'healthy school' in respect of **relations** between staff and pupils and between the pupils themselves? Is the right of all pupils to be treated with respect adequately safeguarded?

☐ Do all the children have appropriate opportunities to contribute to the development of school policy and school life generally? Do all the stakeholders have the chance to be involved in discussion and development of school policy?

School ethos

 Does an **ethos of respect** for human rights, pluralism, justice and democracy (participation) permeate all aspects of school life?

 Is an attitude of respect and partnership extended to the children and all those involved in caring for them?

☐ Do the school's values reflect a proper concern for the **environment** and sustainable development?

Community involvement

 Does the school encourage **positive contact with parents** over the children's need for a clear framework of values and consistent messages about behaviour and discipline? Would it be useful to involve parents in the development and implementation of the school's policy for citizenship education? Are there ways in which parents can share activities with teachers (such as reading about and discussing issues at home)?

 Does the curriculum provide opportunities to invite **visitors from the community** to talk about their work? Are the visits well prepared for? Are the children involved in setting the agenda and making visitors feel welcome?

☐ Are there opportunities in the community to enhance the children's citizenship learning?

☐ Does the school's **extra-curricular** provision encourage children to become actively involved in community projects? Is there a local civic award scheme for primary children[1]?

43

GIVING PUPILS A SAY IN SCHOOL LIFE[2]

As a result of a growing acknowledgement of children's rights to be heard in situations where their interests are affected, the value of involving even young children in the running of the school community is increasingly recognised and appreciated.

In recent years, significant progress has been made towards involving children in areas such as: appraising their learning, addressing problems of loneliness and bullying, resolving conflicts, selecting new staff, and improving the school's physical environment. One of the major tools available to schools in this context is the *school council*.

On the video, Section 4, *A Better Place*, looks in some detail at two primary school councils in action and also draws on the experience of councillors from a third school. The meetings are seen to elicit children's views which the teachers rightfully take into account. They also clearly demonstrate that in many issues the children themselves are the experts. For example, see how much the children of Wheatcroft School contribute to the discussion of how new cloakroom arrangements are working and which issues remain unresolved for some of them.

School councils have the potential to include all pupils in the life of the school through class discussions of issues to be raised in council meetings. This implies that all members of staff, as well as non-teaching staff and governors, should encourage pupil participation and, when appropriate, themselves become involved in the work of the school council.

Benefits to the children

Through involvement in a school council, children can gain:

- a better understanding of their problems
- a say in matters which concern them
- opportunities to learn about the way organisations function, including how resources are deployed and shared problems are addressed

- increased self-confidence in tackling issues, being proactive, speaking in public, debating issues and handling matters in a business-like manner
- opportunities to become more socially and morally responsible
- a greater sense of community across all the school years
- a practical chance to plan for change and see the benefits in reality
- increased self-esteem.

Prof. Lynn Davies[3] of Birmingham University claims that schools with effective councils tend to be more inclusive. Her study suggests that school councils can contribute to an environment in which there is increased peer support for difficult children, and an increased ownership of codes of conduct, thereby exerting positive peer pressure. School councils can assist in identifying ways of minimising the kind of behaviour that leads to exclusion, and can contribute to a more caring and inclusive environment across the school.

Benefits to the school

Schools as a whole gain from having a school council. Some of the benefits they bring are:

- greater awareness of pupil issues and of the realities of the school experience
- greater pupil involvement in school affairs as pupils assist in the implementation of school policy
- harnessing of pupil energy and enthusiasm, such as in fund-raising and organising events
- increased pupil responsibility and ownership of the school, including the grounds and shared property

- school policies that are better grounded in pupil realities
- established consultation procedures to facilitate good and efficient decision making

Setting up a school council

In setting up a school council the following key questions need to be addressed:

What is the best structure for a school council?

In most schools, children from each class elect two councillors (often a boy and a girl) to be their representatives for either one term or one year. Electing a new representative each term extends the opportunity to gain from the experience to more of the children.

Ability is one criterion for election but probably more important are **reliability** and a **sense of responsibility**. All children who stand for election must be made aware of what they are taking on. Many schools provide training for councillors once they are elected.

Some schools do not involve the very youngest children but many do, including those from reception classes. It seems better to assume that **all** age groups should be represented.

Who should attend the school council?

Adults should not be seen or felt to dominate the school council. However, it is important to involve adults other than the teaching staff. Many intractable problems of school life tend to involve lunch-time supervisors, caretakers, governors and parents as much as they do teachers and children.

It is usual to appoint a member of staff as a **link teacher**. Serious consideration should be given to writing this responsibility into the relevant job description as it should never be undertaken half-heartedly. The link teacher will:

- act as mentor and trainer to the children
- give advice and information but not dictate the council's decisions
- assist the children between meetings to carry out any designated tasks and to prepare for the next meeting
- act as a close link with the head, who may or may not attend all council meetings
- act as a point of reference for other staff on council matters, encouraging good feedback to the whole school.

Outside visitors, including local councillors, police officers or road safety officers, might be invited to attend the school council from time to time, as appropriate. In addition, members of the school council might visit the local council chamber and/or local charities supported by the school.

How often should the school council meet?

Having too many meetings can cause fatigue and a sense of time-wasting. Too few meetings can result in a failure to create a sense of involvement and momentum for the children. When intervals between meetings are too long, the business of the school council and pupil participation may be forgotten about and a sense of disillusionment replace the initial enthusiasm.

Meetings need to take place regularly (perhaps every two or three weeks) and not be cancelled, except in extreme circumstances.

If attending every meeting is a problem for anyone attending *ex officio*, such as a governor or caretaker, they might be able to regularly attend every other meeting or when their presence is specifically relevant.

Sub-committees might be appointed to carry business forward between meetings. For example, to gather ideas for the designated school charities or to process pupil questionnaires.

All staff need to be aware of when meetings will take place in order to hold the necessary preparatory class council or Circle Time sessions.

Meetings of the school council need to be well publicised in the staff room and in assembly. The minutes of each meeting should be made widely available and, as a matter of routine, disseminated to all the children.

Should the school council have its own budget?

The greater the sense of responsibility felt by the councillors, the better. Money might be allocated to the council to spend on play equipment or the school environment. If children have been involved in fund-raising, they might reasonably expect to have a say, if not the final decision, in how it should be spent. Some schools offer incentives to the children by promising to increase their budget if, for example, vandalism around the school is reduced.

Dummy! That won't get us a new camcorder.

SCHOOLS, CHILDREN AND PARENTS[4]

Establishing the most productive partnership between school and the parents and carers of children is vital. Relations between home and school are complex, not least because of the possible differences in values – an area of particular significance to citizenship education.

Values play an important part in influencing behaviour. For some children, these values are made explicit and are consciously taught. For others, the values are implicit, unexamined and unrecognised. Growing children readily absorb prevailing values, and displaying them in their own thinking and behaviour is one way in which they can confirm their membership of a group.

Public and private values

Homes are private places with their own value systems – some clearer, more articulated and consistent than others. Schools, particularly state-run non-religious schools, are pluralist communities, based on a 'public ethic' of values, such as **equality of opportunity, social justice, non-violence** and **respect for difference**. In addition to these public values, children at school are inevitably exposed to a wide variety of other people's private values, especially those of the other children.

At school, children often experience clashes of values, some of which cause them considerable anguish and uncertainty. It can be difficult in a school to impart values of consideration and respect for others if such values are not the norm in the homes of the children.

On the other hand, many parents are anxious about the kinds of values to which their children are exposed at school and see it as a source of 'contamination'. Children may pick up forbidden knowledge, bad habits and language from their peers, but the **curriculum** itself can also cause conflict between home and school. It encourages children to absorb values or beliefs that some parents feel undermine their own religious, cultural or moral values. Schools need to be sensitive to the perfectly proper anxieties of parents, while encouraging open-mindedness and respect for different cultures, religions and lifestyles.

This distinction between public and private is useful for teachers. School is highly significant in the development of children as social beings. It is where most of them learn the distinction between personal values and the values that underpin the public life of a community. Whilst our **primary relationships** with relations and close friends are based on degrees of love and affection, our **secondary relationships**, with non-intimates, need to be underpinned with different notions, such as rights, respect and fairness. We may not like some people but, nevertheless, they deserve our respect as human beings. Such values need to be taught and learnt (often painfully slowly) and schools make a significant contribution to the process.

All citizens in a democratic society face tensions between these overlapping private and public domains. Some groups or individuals resolve the conflict by turning their back on public life. However, the involved citizen is one who learns to hold both sets of values in creative tension, recognising the importance of engagement even though it may result in compromise and frustration.

QUESTION, THINK, DISCUSS

The National Curriculum non-statutory guidance on citizenship and PSHE rests on the assumption that effective citizenship education is built around encouraging even very young children to **question, think critically** and **discuss issues** of public (community) concern. Such discussions always highlight a mixture of private and public values. The more clearly children are helped to distinguish between them, the easier they will find it to live with a plurality of value systems.

Parenting styles

Piaget[5] saw the role of parents as keeping children in a position of immature morality (see Chapter 1) because their position of moral authority suppressed the child's own thinking. However, recent research has shown that parents adopt a wide range of parenting strategies, besides assertion, and there are now clear pointers as to which of them positively influence moral development.

Several recent studies indicate that where parents discuss the effects of their children's actions on others, are affectionate and responsive, and adopt a democratic (negotiating) style of discipline, the children are more likely to display higher levels of moral maturity.

Parental influence

Walker and Hennig[6] studied the way parents discuss moral issues with their offspring, looking for positive factors such as supportiveness, reasonableness, humour and the mutual sharing of opinions. However, some parents displayed negative attitudes towards their children in discussion, including undermining their self-esteem, or devaluing or distorting the child's contribution. Lack of affection and even hostility were also observed.

The results of this experiment clearly showed that children who displayed the most mature moral judgements (i.e. the least egocentric and the most outwardly considerate) had parents who were much more likely to be warm, supportive, and willing to engage in discussion. Such parents intuitively adjusted their moral reasoning to a level somewhat (but not too much) above their children's current level of moral thinking so as to encourage progression and development. These findings were confirmed by a later study which also found that parents who were personally defensive, rigid, insensitive and emotionally immature inhibited their children's moral development.

If, as research suggests, the more obvious moral characteristics of empathy, conscience and moral reasoning, and factors such as self-esteem and self-control are strongly influenced by parenting, it is essential that we try to unite home and school in developing a better understanding of how each can most effectively contribute to the moral and social development of the children.

DIFFERENCES IN PARENTING

The development of children's moral reasoning is influenced by patterns of communication within the family, including the way discipline is achieved. Parents tend towards one of three different styles in establishing rules and boundaries within the family.

Autocratic

The autocratic style is often associated with fixed rules and rigid boundaries and allows little discussion or compromise when disputes arise. It can provide a certain level of security but does not generally allow children to think for themselves or act on their own initiative. Sanctions may be arbitrary and severe. Relationships between parents and children may be emotionally rather distant but there may be other reasons for the rigidity, such as a strong moral or religious framework to which children are expected to adhere without question.

A disadvantage of this parenting style is that the child may eventually rebel and the child/parent relationship may not be flexible or strong enough to allow a more egalitarian relationship. Away from the fear of such sanctions, some children can become uncontrollable.

Permissive

Characterised by a virtual absence of boundaries and rules, permissive parenting can occasionally swing to the autocratic extreme if the parent becomes anxious about losing control. This can engender insecurity and fails to present children with the idea that certain ways of behaving are unacceptable. This is especially important for children in the early years when they look to external sources of authority to establish boundaries. One danger of this approach is that the child's behaviour may become extreme in an attempt to force the parents to establish clear boundaries.

Democratic

The democratic approach generally offers a limited number of firm boundaries and rules but they are usually negotiable and often incorporate notions of mutual rights and responsibilities. There is clear respect for the feelings of both sides from which children can more easily learn, both by example and clear direction, to empathise with others and thus be more sensitive to the consequences of their own actions. They learn to take responsibility for their own behaviour, to take risks and make choices even if this involves some mistakes along the way.

This parenting style requires more effort, at least at first, and for some parents may feel like a loss of control. However, parenting is a long-term venture and the gradual transfer of responsibilities to the child tends to minimise clashes as the child grows older and the fundamental open relationship remains warm and close. The flexibility built into the relationship allows the balance of power to shift gradually and naturally towards the children as they become increasingly able to accept responsibility for their own actions. If nurtured in the early years, the capacity within a relationship to resolve problems by talking about them, comes into its own during adolescence.

Effective parenting

Parenting which broadly adopts a democratic style is more likely to encourage the development of self-esteem, self-confidence, self-reliance and responsibility – some of the key 'building blocks of morality'.

Parenting is likely to be most effective when:

- children feel secure and loved
- rules are consistent, fair and understood
- rules can be justified when challenged but also be modified by agreement
- discussion is warm, open and two-way, with both sides able to have their point of view heard and respected
- children are encouraged to take as much responsibility for their actions as they are able.

TEACHING STYLES

Teachers and parents have similar concerns for the social and moral development of the children in their care. As with parenting, a democratic, rather than autocratic, teaching approach is more likely to encourage responsible behaviour.

These common concerns for the children's welfare are central to the teacher's task of working out the most constructive and sympathetic way of involving parents in social and moral education.

Dialogue and discussion with children which recognises the importance of **respectful listening** and **equal opportunity to contribute** is the most effective approach to citizenship education. It builds self-confidence, self-esteem, empathy, responsibility and critical thinking. Schools could, therefore, indicate to parents the value of adopting a similar and collaborative approach. This is especially important in creating an open school climate for the discussion of values and attitudes.

Whole school framework

Within the framework of an overall school policy, the individual teacher's work on moral development will be enhanced by a consistent approach throughout the school.

There is increasing emphasis on formalising arrangements with parents through home/school agreements (HSAs). The guidance for drawing up the home/school agreements suggests they should be regarded as one element in a whole school policy for involving parents in a range of issues, including homework, discipline, information exchange and attendance. This could be a vital point of contact for teachers wishing to develop parental involvement in citizenship education.

TEACHERS AND PARENTS WORKING TOGETHER

The elements of citizenship education on which teachers and parents can usefully work together and support one another include the following practical examples.

Rules and boundaries

Since family rules and boundaries are generally the manifestation of different underlying values, there may be wide variations in the rules laid down for different children in any one school.

The important factor in relation to citizenship education is that teachers and parents adopt a consistent approach to those **Key rules** which are about **public behaviour**, such as how children behave towards each other in the playground.

Different methods of making and enforcing rules can be examined, with **differences between home and school** explicitly considered.

The whole notion of **fairness in rule-making** could be considered as part of any discussion about how rules and boundaries are set and enforced. Young children will already think in complex ways about such issues. For example, as long as the reasons are explained, they usually accept that there can be different rules for their older or younger siblings.

Talking about and comparing **how and why home and school rules differ** can help children to understand the need for them and to develop more positive strategies for living with both. The conflict between different sets of rules can be confusing. For example, some parents encourage their children to retaliate in kind if they are hit at school, whilst teachers explicitly forbid it.

Stories are often the best way to introduce such issues (see Chapter 3). For example, in *You, Me, Us!* one story tells of a girl whose teacher has expressed values that are different from those of her home. Class discussion of the story could be followed up by asking the children to talk with their parents about **rules at home and school**, thinking about why rules are there, why they sometimes change, and possibly comparing current rules with those that existed when parents and grandparents were young.

A fruitful discussion of **rules and boundaries** can be built around which **television programmes** the children are permitted to watch at home – an issue on which parents differ greatly. Research has shown that children benefit from being able to talk about such issues. The *Thinkers* picture book *The Scary Video* has been specially written to encourage discussion of this sensitive area.

Talking about rules

The following conversation, which took place between a Year 4 boy and his teacher during a citizenship session, demonstrates the value of talking about such issues.

Aaron:	I know a rule that isn't fair.
Teacher:	Which one is that, Aaron?
Aaron:	The one that says if someone hits you, you are not allowed to hit them back.
Teacher:	Why do you think that's unfair?
Aaron:	Well, if you hit them back they leave you alone.
Teacher:	What happens when you hit them?
Aaron:	They hit you back.
Teacher:	What happens then?
Aaron:	You hit them again.
Teacher:	And then what have you got?
Aaron:	A fight.
Teacher:	What would happen if everyone did that?
William:	It would be chaos!
Aaron *[after thinking for a few seconds]*:	It might not be a fair rule but it's probably a good one because teachers have to look after you and teach you.

Respect for people's differences

This highly sensitive area is at the heart of citizenship education. It is probably the most difficult to address because it is linked into underlying attitudes of which people may scarcely be conscious.

Demonstrating that the **school is an inclusive community** which respects the rights of all its members is paramount and generally achieved by the way people in it behave towards each other. But to assist the assimilation of such values and to help the children deal with life outside of the school gates, the issues need to be explicitly talked about. Involving parents in this dialogue may be an important factor in whether or not it succeeds. Some ways to involve parents include:

- the use of relevant stories to be read at home with parents; this could include picture books without words for younger children
- worksheets to spark off talking and listening at home
- adopting one **key value** every month. **Respect** could be one of the many such concepts that relate to **respecting difference**.

Learning to be responsible

While both school and home provide many opportunities for children to take on various kinds of responsibilities, it is sometimes easier for children to take risks and make mistakes within the secure and private setting of the family. However, there are several ways in which home and school can work together to give children the chance to be depended on, including:

- involving the parents with the children in fundraising for the school or for a designated charity.

- asking the children to discuss with their parents some local issues, such as road safety problems at home time. The children can then report back to class or school councils.

- looking after class pets. Parents may not want or feel able to have a pet full-time but they could help and encourage a child to look after one temporarily. Try to help reluctant parents understand the importance of children learning to be responsible.

Speaking and listening

This is possibly the area in which strong home-school cooperation can be of the greatest benefit to children. School offers many opportunities for speaking and listening, including in Circle Time and class discussions. Ideally, such discussions should be characterised by **reflective and exploratory talk**, qualities that can be very effectively reinforced at home.

For many reasons, some parents may find it hard to find the time to give their attention to discussing issues with their children but if they can be persuaded of its importance their input and support can have a hugely positive effect. Schools and individual teachers can help by taking every opportunity to talk about it with parents and by trying to involve them in inquiry-based discussion work that the children are asked to do at home.

Some suggestions for involving families are:

- Focus on television programmes as a basis for a piece of investigative work that might involve not just parents but the wider family.

- Home-school worksheets which ask questions about non-threatening areas can produce very positive responses.
- Use reading partnership schemes to involve parents more closely in their children's listening and talking. Citizenship issues could regularly feature in such stories and be profitably talked about at home and at school.

Some parents may choose not to become involved or lack the necessary confidence to take on the role being asked of them. To encourage and support them, try having an introductory session at school to outline the value of working together on areas of citizenship education, or run some discussion sessions on particular topics.

Alternatively, you could write to all the parents, setting out the PSHE and Citizenship programmes of study and inviting questions. There are also **organised courses for parents** which can be facilitated or provided by the school. For further information, see Appendix III, page 72.

5. TEACHING AND LEARNING STYLES

USING THE VIDEO CASE STUDIES

The video programme is for use by individual teachers and also as a practical stimulus for group discussion among staff. It shows examples of real teaching in practice, but these videotaped sessions are not meant to be seen as demonstration lessons. This chapter offers a range of critical questions through which the video can be approached, together with suggestions for how the material might be interpreted in the light of these questions.

The teachers shown in the first three sections of the video were asked to take a story and conduct some citizenship work with the children in their own way. They were each provided with a framework of suggested questions but were free to use them in whatever way they chose. The final section shows two school councils at work and

draws on the experience of a third through the eyes of two of its Year 6 members. Each of the four sections of the video programme runs for about fifteen minutes and provides a genuine sense of the atmosphere of the lesson and the teacher's way of working. The extended extracts allow time to examine the children's responses in some detail, especially in terms of their **social and moral development** and their **thinking, speaking and listening skills**.

Each section of the video relates to the discussions in the earlier chapters of this handbook. For example, Section 1, *The Citizenship Circle*, relates particularly to the material on the moral development of the child and provides many good examples of the developmental stage at which many children in the upper primary school are to be found. The extended lesson extract also demonstrates the wide range of functions that questions can perform. This is discussed more fully in Chapter 2 of this handbook to which cross-references are given at appropriate points.

Each of the video extracts raises different issues for consideration. This is not to say, of course, that they cannot be used for other purposes. For example, Sections 1 and 2 both show different teachers using the same material with their classes, each in their own way. In Section 2, the classes are of different age groups, so look for ways in which the older children may have developed in their understanding of the issues.

The video provides opportunities to **compare and contrast** the effectiveness of different **teaching approaches** and examine the different kinds of **response** from the children, especially in terms of their social and moral development and in the light of the need to develop thinking, speaking and listening skills. Whether the differences are due to the individual personality or background of the children, their age, or the approach of the teacher is worth considering.

FOCUS ON VIDEO CONTENT

A look in detail at the four sections of the video.

For each section of the video this chapter will summarise its intention, content, and some of the issues being addressed. It will then suggest some areas on which to focus as you watch the video and provide a commentary on what happens in each lesson from these perspectives. It suggests some of the responses these questions might elicit and indicates what other functions are performed by the questions asked in the videotaped discussions.

If the video is to be used in training sessions with students or colleagues it may be helpful to split into groups, with each small group focusing on one aspect of the lesson and providing feedback for discussion in a plenary session afterwards.

The video programme aims to:

- provide real examples of how citizenship issues can be addressed within the curriculum and as part of the life of the whole school
- provide opportunities to examine the way children think about and discuss social and moral issues
- look at teaching techniques that promote better thinking, speaking and listening
- offer examples of different teaching styles.

VIDEO, SECTION 1 THE CITIZENSHIP CIRCLE

Two teachers work with their Year 6 classes on a story, *A Problem for Mr and Mrs Shah*, from *You, Me, Us!*[1] This provides an opportunity to examine a range of discussion techniques and to examine the way children at the top end of Key Stage 2 think about issues of right and wrong, law breaking, punishment, guilt and responsibility.

The lesson shown is the second of two in which the same story was discussed. After the first lesson, the children had completed a questionnaire (see Appendix II) about the issues in the story.

Notice that the main extract is followed by a shorter extract from the parallel class in the same school. This extract provides further material for analysis and is particularly interesting for the way in which the children draw on their own experiences in discussion.

Starting point: a story

A Problem for Mr and Mrs Shah

Mr Shah doesn't know what to do. Some of the local schoolchildren are stealing from his shop. He doesn't want to involve the police or get the children into serious trouble. Besides, he knows that one of the children, Jimmy Spicer, goes to school hungry, so is he really to blame?

Mrs Shah thinks the police should be told and the children punished. She is aware that the cost of small amounts stolen soon adds up to a much larger sum. Alternatively, they could stop selling sweets but Mr Shah loves having children in his shop and would be very reluctant to adopt this solution.

Questions to consider

How many different issues were discussed during the lesson/s? What were they? Were other important issues *not* discussed?

The issues raised include:
- the morality of stealing
- why children steal
- the age at which one becomes responsible for one's actions
- the seriousness of stealing a small amount
- peer pressure
- the consequences of stealing: (a) for children and (b) for the victims
- the feelings of victims of crime
- how to stop children from stealing (do they need punishment or help?)
- the importance of trust
- the role of parents
- the nature or function of different punishments.

The discussions could also have addressed the issue of stealing as a school problem and how it could be tackled cooperatively. This important theme was touched on but not developed.

How did the teacher try to deepen the children's thinking and understanding of the issues? What kinds of questions were used?

The teacher attempted to deepen the children's thinking and understanding by asking a wide range of open-ended questions that required judgement, not recall. The questions also performed a variety of different functions, including:

[1.50] 'What are the issues?'
(Encouraging analytical thinking)

[1.55] 'What are the points the author is trying to bring up?'
(Analysis, drawing on literacy skills)

[3.28] 'Is it wrong to steal something?'
(Encouraging moral thinking)

[3.52] 'Would it make it OK to steal, then, if you don't have any money?'
(Challenging the child's statement; examining mitigating circumstances)

[4.53] 'I want you to think about yourselves when you've done something wrong at home or at school. What would be the most effective way to stop you from doing that thing?'
(Encouraging reflection on personal experiences)

[6.51] 'Do you think when they are shoplifting, they are doing it personally to Mr Shah?'
(Focusing on a key issue relating to shoplifting)

[7.17] 'Does anybody else agree with Lisa?'
(Throwing the debate back to the children to encourage cross-class exchange; establishing the depth of a consensus and identifying where the agreements/disagreements are)

[8.21] 'Who doesn't care?'
(Encouraging clarity of expression)

[10.06] 'Trust – that's important. Does anybody want to say anything about trust?'
(Picking up on or underlining key words or ideas introduced by the children and opening them up for discussion. This also happened with the significant discussion on parents in this lesson)

[10.43] 'I want you to think about what you would say to persuade these children to stop...'
(Asking the children to utilise their own experience and moral thinking)

[11.21] 'I think I would try and tell the children to think about other people's feelings.'
(Modelling reflective and empathic thinking)

[12.16] 'We've looked at some of the issues of stealing – is it wrong to steal? ...'
(Providing a summary of the discussion at the end)

[14.36] 'I would like everybody to think of a reason why people steal.'
(Going round the circle to encourage maximum participation and underline the importance of everyone's contribution; supporting quieter members of the class)

[16.29] 'I read your questionnaires and most people had put down the fact that they didn't think stealing was a very good idea. Would anyone like to discuss that?'
(Using a questionnaire to elicit a wider range of views than is possible in a discussion, also enables quieter members of the class to contribute)

[20.46] 'So, if they are young children, when is it time to start telling them that people get hurt?'
(Encouraging a pupil to think her statement through a little further)

[21.02] 'I've been asking a lot of questions this morning. Now it's your chance to think of any questions you would like to ask.'
(Encouraging the children to take ownership of discussion questions; acknowledges the reality of the children's experiences; gives the children practice at framing questions for themselves – a task usually monopolised by the teacher)

[21.41] 'What do you think would be the best way of coping with that? Has anyone got any ideas?'
(Teacher refuses to be the expert and takes the children's own experiences seriously, encouraging the children to help each other address common problems)

What other techniques proved to be useful in supporting the children's thinking?

It is worth noting that at no point did the teachers put down the children, correct any of their comments, or re-phrase them into what they as teachers thought they should have said. Such re-shaping of children's comments is a common feature of the way some teachers work[2] and is in evidence elsewhere on this video.

Was there any evidence that the children were genuinely thinking for themselves (i.e. critically)? How far did the children draw on or respond to the ideas of other children? In what ways did they do this? To what extent was the lesson led by either the teacher's or the children's agenda?

There are many instances of the children offering their own ideas or drawing on the ideas of others to take the class's collective thinking much further than it would otherwise have gone. Here are some of them:

[9.02] 'I think the shopkeepers, or the children's parents, should take their children to a man or woman who has been a criminal since they were also children and the man or woman should explain to them what they were doing wrong.'

After this idea was introduced, the next six or seven contributions were all about parents as an important factor in offending situations. The teacher acknowledged this as an idea she herself had not thought of.

[17.28] 'I don't think there's no reason for stealing at any time... so you should never steal even if you've got, like Leah said, even if you ain't got no money...'
(Agreeing and disagreeing with other children's contributions)

[18.40] 'Like Ella said, people who steal a large amount of money are greedy.'
(Agreeing with other children's contributions)

[19.14] 'I know how Mr Shah feels because I have had two things stolen from me...'
(Making an original contribution based on personal experience, introducing the idea of trust which was new to this discussion)

[20.20] 'I think it's different when, like, young people steal and old people steal... because little children don't know what they're doing.'
(This was a new idea which was acknowledged by the teacher who then asked a probing question in clarification. Unfortunately, perhaps, this discussion was foreclosed when the teacher moved swiftly on.)

What evidence on video shows *how* the children were thinking about moral issues (including issues of right and wrong, being good or bad, law breaking, guilt, responsibility and punishment)? In what ways is this different from the way an adult might consider the same issues?

Children in the primary years can be seen to think in distinctive and recognisable ways about moral issues (see Chapter 1). Examples of children thinking this way in the video programme include:

[4.20] 'If you steal something little, when you get older you get away with it, you'll steal even bigger things, like cars.'
(There is little sense here that people can learn from their own mistakes, or grow out of offending)

[5.27] 'I think that the best way to stop me playing my music too loud is taking my CD player away.'
(A not uncommon suggestion from a young person that they cannot control their own behaviour and look to adults to do so)

[9.51] 'If I was the parent I would be furious that my child was stealing and I would ground them for a year.'
(A good example of the punishment-orientated stage of moral thinking – this level of draconian strictness is common in children of this age)

[18.12] 'It doesn't matter how much it is but it would be better if they only stole a little thing, because they would maybe get in less trouble.'
(Note the egocentric concern for the offender and the lack of thought for the victims)

At the top end of the primary school, many children are becoming more empathic in their understanding of others' thoughts and feelings, enabling them to develop a more mature understanding of why people behave in the way they do and of the negative consequences of offending behaviour. Moral concerns become more 'person orientated' and less 'authority orientated'. Some of the children in the lesson display this wider, more caring perspective:

[5.43] '[You should] do something to the person you have done something wrong to, to make up for what you have done.'
(Reparation is as important or better than punishment, as it recognises the needs of the victim)

[6.35] 'It probably meant a lot to him [Mr Shah] that the children kept on coming into his shop and buying stuff and then he finds out that they're stealing from him and he probably wants to know why they are doing it.'
(Well developed insights into the thoughts and feelings of others)

[6.56] 'There might be something wrong at home or something that the person's feeling inside...'
(More developed understanding of the inner causes of bad behaviour)

How does the teacher encourage empathic awareness and encourage the sharing of personal experiences to promote community building?

The teacher helps to promote empathy in the lesson in several ways, including:

[6.26] 'Put yourself in Mr Shah's place. How do you think Mr Shah would feel then if he thinks these children are his friends and they are stealing things from him?'
(Asking the children to consider their own or others' feelings)

[7.18] 'I know I've had things stolen from me...'
(Encouraging the children to talk about personal feelings and experiences promotes understanding of other people's inner states)

[8.30] 'Who else could you feel sorry for in this story?'
(An excellent question, provoking rich and varied responses)

[11.11] 'I think I would try and tell the children to think about others' feelings...'
(Here, in the round, the teacher participates at the same level as the children and models for them reflective and caring thinking)

VIDEO, SECTION 2 WEIGHING THE EVIDENCE

The video shows two teachers using a *Thinkers* picture book, each with their own Year 1 and Year 4 class. This provides an opportunity to compare the thinking of children of different ages, and examine different discussion techniques, including different forms of questioning. The lessons also demonstrate different ways in which democratic votes can be taken on an issue and drawn on in the subsequent discussion. The story itself raises issues of fairness, loyalty, kindness and the conflict between duty and personal pleasure.

Starting point: a *Thinkers* story

The Sand Tray

Johnny and his best school friend Tim are making up a story in the sand tray when the teacher approaches them with Kylie, who is feeling left out. The teacher asks the two boys to allow Kylie to join in with them.

Johnny often plays with Kylie out of school but today he is torn between his desire to play **only** with Tim and his duty to include Kylie in the game.

Johnny's duty (though he does not see it this way) arises from three different factors:
• he often plays with Kylie at home, so not to play with her would be unkind and inconsistent
• Kylie is unhappy and lonely, and Johnny has it in his power to cheer her up
• the teacher has asked him to play with Kylie.

Questions to consider

You can use any of the questions suggested for Section 1 of the video to consider the key issues. This story also lends itself to discussion of other matters, including the following.

Fairness is central to living together in society and is of concern to children at every stage of their development. List all the fairness issues raised by this short story. How many of them are addressed directly or indirectly on video? What other issues could arise from this story?

Examples of fairness issues include:
• Was Johnny unfair to Kylie by not playing with her in school when he often does so at home? Should he feel an obligation to Kylie? Is it unfair to treat people inconsistently?
• Were Johnny and Tim unfair to Kylie as someone in distress? Shouldn't they try to help people who are sad or lonely if they can? Wouldn't they expect someone to do this for them? If so, shouldn't they do it for others?

• Was Mrs Peters unfair to Johnny and Tim in asking them to allow Kylie to join in? Why did Mrs Peters do this?
• Was Kylie being fair to Johnny and Tim in expecting them to allow her to join in? Shouldn't she have waited for them to finish the game? In what other ways was Kylie unfair to the boys?
• Were Johnny and Tim treated fairly in the end by Mrs Peters?
• Was Kylie fairly treated?

Other issues that arise from the story include:
• The nature of our obligations to others, namely: best friends, other friends, teachers
• The nature of friendship itself, including what we should look for in a friend
• Why do we have classroom rules about sharing? In what ways is the classroom different from a private place, such as one's home?

How did the teachers focus on areas of disagreement amongst the children? Compare, for example, the different ways in which they used the results of the class votes. How far do you agree with teachers who feel that Key Stage 1 children are too young to deal with value conflict? Is this supported by the video evidence?

The teachers dealt with the vote in different ways, including:

Chris Jay, Year 1, took a vote on whether Johnny's action was right or wrong, then she asked the children to predict the outcome of the vote and explain their thinking.

Angela Bonsar, Year 4, took a vote on whether Kylie should be allowed to play now or wait until the boys had finished their game. Discussion pursued the majority line.

Angela Bonsar also asked the children about the nature of friendship, for example: What makes a friend? Can anyone be your friend? What did it feel like when you had no friends? (Directed to one pupil.)

In a recent piece of research Annabelle Dixon[3] found that many primary heads felt the discussion of contested ideas was not appropriate for children in Key Stage 1. As one head put it, 'Key Stage 1 is for learning rules, not learning to think.' How far is this contradicted by the video evidence and your own experience?

Using the categories open questions and closed questions, note down any examples used by the teachers. Compare their different functions and the advantages and disadvantages of using open and closed types of question in citizenship work.
Open and closed questions used included:

Chris Jay with Year 1:
[22.48] 'Why did she want to play with Johnny?'

[23.53] 'I just want you to think in your heads if Johnny was right to say no, or was he wrong to say no.'

[25.40] 'I wonder if someone can tell me why they thought Johnny was wrong.'

[26.41] 'Is it OK sometimes to tell someone you don't want to be someone's friend?'

[27.17] 'How could he have done that? Can you think of a way?'

Angela Bonsar with Year 4:
[28.20] 'Who can tell me what Johnny's problem was?'

[29.35] 'Do you think he'd got two problems really or one problem?'

[30.18] 'Who thinks Johnny should let Kylie play? And who thinks Kylie should wait?'

[33.12] 'Can *anybody* be your friend?'

[33.36] 'Why can't anybody be your friend?'

Compare the advantages and disadvantages of having the children:
a. clustered around the teacher
b. sitting in a circle.
Relate what you see on the video to your own experience. Do you strongly favour one method over the other? Is there an advantage in varying your practice or is it better to stick to a familiar routine?

Factors include:
- for younger children, a circle can sometimes seem dauntingly large and they sometimes find it hard to make themselves heard
- clustering children means they see very few faces
- clusters of children may focus attention on the teacher and away from other speakers
- the circle encourages exchanges between pupils
- using the 'round' as a technique is difficult if the children are not in a circle
- children learn that being in the circle means different ground rules for discussion. This can give the children added self-confidence and enthusiasm. Compare the comments of the children who were in Mark Prentice's lesson (see video, Section 3) about the joy of being able to argue for once: 'You're not usually allowed to argue, are you?'

VIDEO, SECTION 3 READING, THINKING, SPEAKING AND LISTENING

Examining the moral issues that arise from shared texts can draw on techniques familiar to literacy work. The teacher seen in this section of the video uses a popular picture book, *Tusk, Tusk*[4] by David McKee, to generate a very lively discussion around issues of peace and conflict in relation to the individual and groups. The lesson shown was the third one based on this book. As the teacher, Mark Prentice, was working with a class that was not his own the children wore name tags.

Starting point: a story

Tusk, Tusk

Two groups of elephants, one black and one white, grow deeply suspicious of one another to the point where war breaks out. Groups of peace-loving elephants from both sides escape into the jungle to avoid the conflict. Long after the black and white elephants have wiped each other out the descendants of the peace-loving elephants re-emerge from the jungle having become grey elephants. For a while, all is well – until it is noticed that some of the elephants are different in other ways and the whole cycle of mistrust and violence threatens to begin again.

Questions to consider

You can use the questions (except the first block) that relate to Section 1 of the video also to review this lesson. In addition, or alternatively, you could consider the following questions.

In terms of teacher input and pupil outcome, compare the lesson in this section with that in Section 2, which is also with a Year 4 class and in a circle. How would you account for the differences between the style and 'feel' of the two lessons?

The differences between the discussions in the two lessons could be considered in terms of:

A teaching styles. For example:
• use of open and closed questions
• the extent to which the teacher determines the direction of the discussion
• the extent to which the children are encouraged to interact with each other
• the use of time for the children to discuss issues in small groups

• the use of 'tool' words (see Chapter 3)
• the extent to which the teacher models reflective language as a participant in the discussion.

B the children's responses. For example:
• length
• spontaneity
• to whom the response was directed.

At the end of the section, Mark Prentice says, **'I don't see myself as teaching moral righteousness but I do see myself as giving children the forum to debate these sorts of issues so that, when they are old enough, they can form opinions for themselves but will have the skills to do so in an informed way.'**

Consider the role of the teacher in developing:
• **children's personal character, including their moral values**
• **children's ability to be 'good citizens'.**

See Chapters 1 and 2 for a discussion of these issues.

Mark suggests that the sharing of personal experience is valuable but it can go too far or become 'self indulgent'. Consider the issues around confidentiality and disclosure in citizenship work. Where are the professional limits to be drawn between work which develops empathy and that which becomes intrusive?

These issues need to be considered in the light of teachers' general responsibility to disclose evidence of abuse to the appropriate member of staff. Teachers are not able to offer complete confidentiality to children or their parents and they are obliged to pass on any information about behaviour which could cause harm to children or others. Teachers are not, however, bound to disclose knowledge of illegal activity, such as a child revealing that members of the family are involved in stealing. The standard is that one should always act in the best interests of the child.

For a full discussion of the treatment of sensitive and controversial issues see the non-statutory guidance for PSHE and Citizenship (DfEE, 2000).

Consider the overlap between citizenship work and the development of literacy, speaking and listening in the context of your own school practices. To what extent is it possible to meet overlapping curriculum objectives at the same time? What are the disadvantages of this?

There are a number of important overlaps between discussion-based citizenship work (as advocated here) and the development of literacy, speaking and listening, and critical thinking. The shared discussion of texts rich in social and moral concerns not only accesses literacy targets but also provides rich opportunities for the children to engage with each other, reflect on their own experience, learn how to publicly argue a case, criticise a point of view, and so on.

In order for literacy work not to become stale, different types of texts should be used, including those where language-based work may feature less prominently than the promotion of discussion and critical thinking.

English work should include regular opportunities for the development of speaking and listening skills in both key stages. The speaking and listening recommendations for 'group discussion' work are very much in line with good citizenship practice, including:

Key Stage 1
- taking turns in speaking
- relating contributions to what has gone before
- taking different views into account
- extending their ideas in the light of discussion
- giving reasons for their opinions and actions

Key Stage 2
- making relevant contributions
- taking turns in discussion
- making exploratory and tentative comments where ideas are being collected together and reasoned evaluative comments as discussion moves to conclusions
- justifying what they think after listening to others
- dealing politely with opposing points of view
- enabling discussion to move on
- reaching agreement, considering alternatives and anticipating consequences.

VIDEO, SECTION 4 A BETTER PLACE

School councils can be an effective way of involving children more closely in the running of the school. This section of the video examines the contribution that young children can make and what issues school councils can realistically address. It shows two school councils at work, and offers perspectives on the work of a third council from two of its Year 6 members. Before watching the video you could think about different reasons for and against having a school council.

Questions to consider

The framework for PSHE and Citizenship suggests that children 'participate... in the school's decision-making processes, relating it to democratic structures and processes.' From what you have seen on the video and from your own experience, consider the learning potential of involvement in class and school councils. To what extent is a school council an *essential element* of a whole school policy for citizenship?

See Chapter 4 for a full discussion of these issues.

What range of issues was discussed on the video? Were any of them surprising or novel? How would these issues relate to your own school?

Most of the issues covered in the two council meetings are indicated by the captions. Also briefly discussed were:
• relations with supply teachers
• play equipment
• parking outside the school
• bullying.

In thinking about how the issues relate to your own school, you might consider:

• [*if you have no council*] does the video suggest that a council could make a useful contribution to the life of the school?
• [*if you already have a council*] how does the scope of issues covered compare with those shown on the video programme?
• What is the value of having adults other than teachers on the school council? Are there arguments against it? Consider all the possibilities.

• How could the children's concerns be classified into groups, such as the school grounds and environment? Consider which of these issues might usefully be discussed with the children in your own school.

In bringing their own experiences to the council, what evidence was there that the children were using their own judgement? How sensible were these judgements? In some areas, the pupils were often the experts and the teachers were learning from them. In what issues was this very clear?

The insights of the children were invaluable in the issues of the cloakrooms, the lost property, and double parking outside school.

Lilian Sanders expressed the hope that the children would one day be able to run the school council themselves. Do you agree? Consider the arguments for and against. Are there any other implications of the children's relative inexperience and immaturity?

The arguments in favour of the children running the school council are likely to be based on the educational benefits of learning to handle complex roles such as those of chair and secretary.

The more self-standing the council becomes, the greater it runs the risk of the issues for discussion being generated only by the children. Compare this with the number of issues on the video which were brought to the council by the staff.

There is always the danger that school councils can degenerate into complaints sessions, particularly if the agenda is not a shared one, with items generated by both staff and children.

All things considered, are you broadly for or against having a school council in your school? List the arguments in favour of having one and the benefits to: (a) the children, and (b) the school. Similarly, list any disadvantages.

What kinds of information are difficult to gather from school councils?

Points raised by councillors might come from class votes or individual suggestions. This can work well for some kinds of issues but is not necessarily the best way to determine whether *all* the children were broadly happy or unhappy with, say, the levels of bullying or racism in the school, nor whether the experience of minority groups in the school differed from that of the majority.

As in many other situations, majority voting can easily obscure, or fail to elicit, much important information. A survey form completed by every child in the school would be a better way to gather the necessary data. Some of this material could be the focus of attention for a small group of senior colleagues, possibly working with members of the governing body as part of the process of developing the school's policy for PSHE and Citizenship.

APPENDIX I

IDEAS FOR TRAINING SESSIONS

The video accompanying this handbook is an ideal resource for group training sessions on education for citizenship. All of the questions suggested for consideration by teachers in Chapter 5 can be addressed. In addition, this appendix provides more exercises and ideas to complement the work based around the video.

As INSET time is limited in primary schools, a training programme might be offered to the whole staff as an introduction to citizenship work. Those interested in taking things further could be invited to form a group that would continue to work through the issues raised by the video and this handbook.

Alternatively, some of this material could be the focus of attention for a small group of senior colleagues, possibly working with members of the governing body as part of the process of developing the school's policy for PSHE and Citizenship.

USING THE VIDEO FOR TRAINING

An effective way to make use of the video material is for colleagues to divide into small groups, each one focusing on a different aspect of the lesson. After viewing the extract, the groups will need some time for discussion before feedback so they can relate their own perceptions to what is generally thought of as good practice or to what is known from research.

As the video shows recognisable and achievable practice (not something fabricated for the camera) it provides an effective link to the relevant theoretical framework of educating for citizenship. This will help teachers make better sense of their own practice and provide them with the tools they need for better planning and management of the learning process.

FURTHER IDEAS

Exercise 1
What kind of citizens do we want to promote?

As a way in to the purpose of citizenship education, ask colleagues to share their ideas about what kind of citizens primary schools ought to promote. The list can be compared with what is in the non-statutory guidance. Teachers tend to be reassured when their own aspirations, such as encouraging respect for others and developing independent thinkers, are reflected in the guidelines, and realise that citizenship education need not be seen as an add-on but as making a vital contribution to children's social and moral development.

Exercise 2
Build a curriculum on key concepts

This exercise helps direct attention to the importance of the key concepts in curriculum planning, lesson delivery and in ensuring continuity and progression across the key stages. Take the key concepts of *justice or fairness*, *rights* and *responsibilities* and look at ways in which they are relevant to the children's experience. For example:

- what issues of fairness would they recognise as significant for themselves or others?
- what rights should they know they have?
- what responsibilities might they be expected to be aware of?
- how do these change or develop as the children grow older?

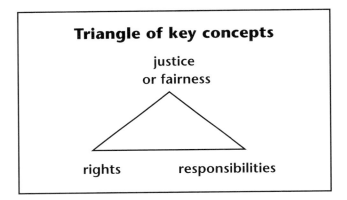

Triangle of key concepts

If time allows, repeat the exercise with some or all of the following concepts, all of which underpin issues of citizenship:

Social concepts

power	cooperation
authority	democracy
rules	diversity (pluralism)
laws	equality
community	inequality
conflict	

Moral (or value) concepts

right
wrong
good
bad

Exercise 3
Exploring stages of moral development

This exercise relates to the discussions of **moral maturity** in Chapter 1 and in Chapter 5 (section 1). It can be instructive for all colleagues to look at the responses of their own class in the light of the shift from **immature to mature moral thinking** (see page 16).

Prior to the training session, ask the participating teachers to do the following exercise with their class and bring along the results for discussion.

Ask the children to think of as many answers as they can to the question:

Why would it be wrong to steal?

An alternative introduction to this whole topic could be to ask colleagues to make a joint list of all the reasons why they think it would be wrong to steal. Compare their answers with those of the children in the light of the developmental model offered (see page 16). Do the results of your survey tend to support this model or not?

This exercise can become bogged down in trying to interpret particular answers. By no means are *all* moral statements 'scoreable', because the children's underlying social awareness is not always made clear. For example, the opinion **you should be kind to others** may look like an empathic statement but it could actually be a rule the child has taken on trust from an adult. It would be necessary to ask the further question: '*Why* do you think it is important to be kind?'

The children might reply in ways which are more revealing of their moral stage, including:

- Because if you're unkind you will get into trouble.
- Because if you're unkind people won't like you.
- Because if you're unkind you hurt other people's feelings and that's horrible for them.

WHY WOULD IT BE WRONG TO STEAL?

As an additional exercise in exploring the stages of moral development, this transcript of a discussion between a teacher and a Year 5 class of ten-year-olds could be used as an example. Ask colleagues to identify children's responses as *immature* or *mature*.

T= teacher   P= pupil

T **Can we think of all the reasons why it might be wrong to steal?**

P1 You might get caught and all your friends might tell on you.

P2 If you are going to steal and someone sees you they might tell the police and you'll get into even worse trouble.

P3 You won't go to heaven, you'll go to hell.

P4 It's better not to steal, you'll just get into trouble and it's better not to.

P5 You'll get a police record and if you're old enough you'll get put in jail.

T **You've given me lots of reasons about why it is better for yourselves but what about the effects on other people?**

P6 Well, if one person steals, others might think it's cool and they'll go stealing and then even more people will go stealing.

P7 If you're caught stealing and they tell your mum, you might get grounded for a week.

T **What other effect might it have on your mum?**

P8 She'll be cross.

P9 She might be upset her daughter is turning into a bad person.

P10 She might think she's been a bad mother.

P11 She might be upset because when she goes into a shop people might think she's going to steal from them. *[Notice the tendency for the children to impute selfish or immature judgements to the mother]*

P12 She might have to pay back the money.

P13 She might feel guilty and embarrassed about her son or daughter going round stealing things.

T **But what about the people you're stealing from? No one has mentioned that. No one has worried about the people who have had something stolen.**

P14 If they've trusted you for years they might be surprised and feel shocked.

P15 If you go in a shop and steal and tell your friends, they might think it's a good idea and they might go into a shop and the shopkeeper might catch them and they'll get into lots of trouble and their mum and dad might feel really angry.

Exercise 4
Using stories to develop critical thinking around citizenship issues

Select a story or picture book, such as one of the *Thinkers* books. Identify the citizenship issues in the story and **frame appropriate questions**. Colleagues could work in their year groups, but there may also be some advantage in teachers of young children working with colleagues from the upper years. Many open-ended questions will be the same for all age groups – the differentiation will be by outcome.

Identify any central issues which should be addressed at all costs. Teachers should keep these in mind and try to ensure they are introduced into the discussion as naturally as possible.

Since questions do many different jobs, consciously try to include a **mixture of question types**, including those that will develop:

- **moral awareness**: the 'rights and wrongs' of situations, moral conflicts, intention, mitigation, consequences and so on.
- **empathic awareness**: feelings, inner thoughts, human character traits and so on.

- **multiple perspective-taking**: both of the above areas should apply to all the major characters in a story.
- **shared experiences and community building**: encouragement of feelings of solidarity, issues of shared concern, belonging and interdependence.
- **social learning**: building on the children's existing knowledge to expand their understanding of how society functions, for example, the role of the police or local government.

Identify some questions for group enquiry (i.e. open to anyone to offer a point of view) and some question stems for going round the circle.

As a follow-up, groups of teachers could select a book they would like to use with their own classes. They could develop a list of useful questions and share their ideas with colleagues. For use in citizenship work, build up a **resource bank** of the books and relevant questions and ideas that have worked well. Indicate the age group for which each one is appropriate. Look for a spread of issues per year group and for the same key concepts to be tackled in each key stage.

APPENDIX II

QUESTIONNAIRE ABOUT MR AND MRS SHAH

From *Critical Thinking in Young Minds* (see page 71, Further Reading).

Name: . . . .   **Year:** . . .   **Age:** . . .   **Y** . . .   **M** . . .   **Date:** . . . .

You are asked a number of questions about the story. After each answer, write 'WHY?' on a new line and give your reason.

1. What is interesting to you about the story? Why?

2. What question would you like to ask about it? Why?

3. What would you do if you saw someone shoplifting? Why?

4. Do you feel sorry for anyone in the story? Why?

5. Is it wrong to steal? Why?

6. Is there any situation a person could be in where they should steal? Give your reason.

7. What do you like about the story? Why?

8. What do you not like about it? Why?

9. Is the story finished? Why do you say that?

10. How should it end? Why?

Appendix III

NOTES, FURTHER INFORMATION, RESOURCES

Chapter 1
Citizenship and the Primary Curriculum

1. Dunn, Judy. *The Beginnings of Social Understanding*, Blackwell, Oxford, 1987, provides a highly readable account of the enormous strides in social understanding and language mastery made by children between the ages of 18 months and 3 years.

2. Cullingford, Cedric. *Children and Society*, Cassell, London, 1992, offers a detailed and fascinating account of how children aged 7–11 think about social issues and of what kind of social knowledge they have accumulated by the time they leave primary school.

3. This scheme is broadly based on the moral stage theory developed by Lawrence Kohlberg, as modified by John Gibbs in *Moral Maturity, measuring the development of Sociomoral Reflection* by Gibbs, Basinger and Fuller, Erlbaum, 1992. Piaget, a pioneer in this field, suggested that the early moral stages were 'heteronomous' or external, whilst the later stages represent an 'autonomous' stage where moral values have become internalised. Gibbs characterised these two stages as 'immature' and 'mature', using Kohlberg's more complex shift through a number of stages demonstrating greater social awareness at each stage. An excellent discussion of the way moral stage theory can be applied to the primary classroom is found in *Moral Classrooms, Moral Children* by Rheta De Vries and Betty Zan, Teachers College Press, New York, 1994.

Chapter 2
The Importance of Talk

1. See David Wood's research on classroom talk and the use of questions in *How Children Think and Learn*, Blackwell, Oxford, 1988.

2. Mercer, Neil. *The Guided Construction of Knowledge*, Multilingual Matters, Clevedon, 1995.

3. SAPERE (Society for the Advancement of Philosophical Enquiry and Reflection in Education) is an organisation that exists to promote critical and philosophical thinking in schools. Besides offering teachers training in how to deepen children's thinking through discussion, SAPERE also runs a website using a different item of news each month to generate discussion. A simplified version of the story is available for primary schools. Notes for the teacher suggest ideas for discussion. The children, if they wish, can engage in debate with children from other schools using the conferencing facility. The address of the website is: www.sapere.net.

4. Gill Rose, as a teacher of a Year 3 class, carried out some action research for an MA in Education at the Roehampton Institute.

Chapter 3
Literacy and Citizenship

1. Tizard, Barbara and Hughes, Martin. *Young Children Learning: talking and thinking at home and at school*, Fontana Press, London, 1984.

2. Lishak, Antony. *Coming Round* is available from the author at 38 Wentworth Road, High Barnet, Herts, EN5 4NT. Telephone: 020 8441 6953. E-mail: anthony@harpo.demon.co.uk.

3. For example, Tuckswood Community First School, Norwich (head teacher: Sue Eagle), has made **philosophy for children** a core element of the curriculum. OFSTED concluded that this had a very positive impact on the quality of learning in the school and on the whole school ethos.

Chapter 4
Whole School Issues

1. A number of areas operate civic award schemes for primary pupils, some modelled on the Duke of Edinburgh's Award Scheme which pupils cannot join until the age of 14. In Southampton, for example, such a scheme is in operation. For more information about how it works, contact Roy Honeybone, Advisory Teacher for Citizenship, Hampshire Inspection and Advisory Service.

2. We have gratefully drawn on the work of Gill Morris, Advisory Teacher for PSHE, Camden, through her booklet *School Councils in Primary Schools. Training Pack 1999*. A useful handbook for children, *The School Council: a children's guide*, draws heavily on the children's own experiences of being councillors, and is available from: Save the Children, Hawthorns House, Halfords Lane, Smethwick, B66 1BB. Telephone: 0121 558 0111.

3. Davies, Lynn. *School Councils and Pupil Exclusions Research Report*, School of Education, University of Birmingham, 1998.

4. In using the term 'parents' we also include carers.

5. Piaget, J. *The Moral Judgement of the Child*, Penguin, Harmondsworth, 1932.

6. Walker, L.J. and Hennig, K.H. 'Parenting Style and the Development of Moral Reasoning', *Journal of Moral Education*, Vol. 28: 3, Carfax., Abingdon, 1999.

7. *You, Me, Us! Education for Social and Moral Responsibility* is a collection of stories for Key Stages 1 and 2, edited by Don Rowe and Jan Newton to support citizenship work in primary schools. Free copies are available to teachers, students and trainers. Details from The Citizenship Foundation, Ferroners House, Shaftesbury Place, off Aldersgate Street, London EC2Y 8AA. Telephone: 020 7367 0500. E-mail: info@citfou.org.uk.

Chapter 5
Teaching and Learning Styles

1. See Note 7 above

2. Edwards, D. and Mercer, N. *Common Knowledge, the development of Understanding in the Classroom*, Routledge, London, 1987.

3. Dixon, A. 'The Preconceptions and Practice in Primary Citizenship Education', *Forum* Volume 41:1, Triangle Journals, Wallingford, Oxfordshire, 1999.

4. McKee, David, *Tusk, Tusk,* Andersen Press (hb), Red Fox (pb).

FURTHER READING

Fisher, Robert. *Teaching Thinking: philosophical enquiry in the classroom*, Cassell, London, 1998.

Murris, K. *Teaching Philosophy with Picture Books*, Infonet Publications, 1992. Details from: Centre for Philosophy with Children, University of Wales.

Prentice, M. *A Community of Enquiry in Talk & Learning: 5–16 Oracy Plan for Teachers in Milton Keynes*, Open University, Milton Keynes, 1991.

Quinn, V. *Critical Thinking in Young Minds*, Fulton, London, 1997.

Ray, C. 'Read All About It! Using children's books in sex and relationships education', *Primary Practice* 21, Nash Pollock, Oxford, 1999.

COURSES FOR PARENTS AND TEACHERS

There is currently a growing emphasis on the importance of education for parenthood in the sense of involving and supporting parents in key aspects of their children's learning and development. Many schools now facilitate or provide such courses for parents. Evaluations, where available, suggest that they provide valuable and welcome support for parents, many of whom express delight in improved communications with their children and a more cooperative atmosphere at home.

Family Links: The Nurturing Programme

This programme has helped reduce depression within participating families, and reduced harsh or ineffective discipline and correspondingly difficult behaviour in children.

Working through schools, the Family Links charity developed a two-pronged approach:

a with all the staff and through teachers with all children in the school, using Circle Time, art and games to encourage the children to recognise and talk about different kinds of feelings, improve their conflict resolution skills, relate and communicate better with others, and so on.

b with groups of self-selected parents meeting separately and following a parallel programme. All parents are invited to attend.

Family Links trains and supports the whole school staff in introducing the ten-week programmes for nursery and Key Stages 1 and 2. They can be contacted at: Family Links, New Marston Centre, Jack Straws Lane, Oxford, OX3 0DL.

Co-operative Kids

School Matters... and so do parents!

These two courses are written by Elizabeth Hartley-Brewer, author of *Positive Parenting* and *Motivating Your Child*. They are specifically designed for use by teachers, parents or other school-based professionals working in partnership to introduce parents to many of the challenging issues surrounding their child's social, emotional and intellectual development.

Co-operative Kids emphasises the importance of positive self-esteem to all aspects of child development, again showing the value of positive expectations, clear boundaries and good communication between children and parents. Difficult areas including managing deadlock and defiance are addressed, with handy hints and summaries available to take away at the end of each session. All parents are encouraged to attend so no stigma can be attached to any particular families. Parents are encouraged to reflect on and share their personal experiences but there is never any pressure on them to disclose anything that might be sensitive or threatening.

School Matters is aimed at parents who want to help their children get the most out of school. It touches on topics such as: homework, coping with the playground, talking with teachers, TV and video games.

Packs for facilitators are available for both courses, as is training. For further details, contact: Elizabeth Hartley-Brewer, 117 Corringham Road, London NW11. Telephone: 020 8458 8404.

Time Out for Parents

This is another Positive Parenting Publications course. It is aimed at parents and can be offered by teachers, health visitors or social workers. Five basic sessions cover: the needs of parents and children, emotional security, listening skills, setting 'loving limits', and talking about sexuality (child protection).

For more details, contact: Positive Parenting Publications, 39 Wallington Road, Copnor, Portsmouth PO2 0HB. Telephone: 023 9250 1111.

INDEX

THINKERS PICTURE BOOKS

JOE'S CAR

Annabelle Dixon and Tim Archbold

Joe's shiny red car is hidden by Charlie and found by Ben; but Joe doesn't respond predictably to either of them.

Key issues: ideas about ownership, respect for property, sharing, honesty, friendship, forgiveness.
ISBN 0-7136-5846-0

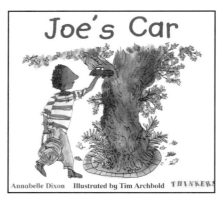

THE SAND TRAY

Don Rowe and Tim Archbold

Johnny is friends with Tim at school and with Kylie when he's at home so why can't the three of them play together in the sand tray?

Key issues: rules, rights, responsibilities, authority, friendship, loyalty, fairness.
ISBN 0-7136-5843-6

THE SCARY VIDEO

Gill Rose and Tim Archbold

Claire is thrilled when the grown-ups don't notice her staying up late to watch a video but then she can't get the scary images out of her head.

Key issues: television-viewing, common dilemma, authority and disobedience, rights, justice or fairness, responsibility, feelings, fear.
ISBN 0-7136-5844-4

WILLIAM AND THE GUINEA-PIG

Gill Rose and Tim Archbold

William finally gets his longed-for pet but does not want to share it with his little sister. Fortunately, Kelly is not easily deterred.

Key issues: family, responsibility, caring for other creatures, forgiveness.
ISBN 0-7136-5837-1

THINKERS ORDER FORM

	ISBN	PRICE	QTY
Joe's Car Annabelle Dixon & Tim Archbold	0 7136 5846 0	£3.99	
The Sand Tray Don Rowe & Tim Archbold	0 7136 5843 6	£3.99	
The Scary Video Gill Rose & Tim Archbold	0 7136 5844 4	£3.99	
William and the Guinea-Pig Gill Rose & Tim Archbold	0 7136 5837 1	£3.99	

Please send me the books listed above.
Postage and packing is FREE within the UK.

☐ I enclose a cheque made payable to A & C Black (Publishers) Ltd for £ _____

☐ Please debit my Mastercard/Visa/Switch account

☐ Please invoice me at the address below.

No: ☐☐☐☐☐☐☐☐☐☐☐☐☐☐☐☐☐☐☐

Expiry Date: ☐☐☐☐   Issue No: ☐☐   Signature: _____

Name _____

Address _____

_____

Postcode _____

Please return your order to:
A & C Black, PO Box 19, St Neots, Cambs PE19 8SF
tel: 01480 212666 fax: 01480 405014 email: sales@acblackdist.co.uk

NOTES

NOTES

NOTES

NOTES